Lady Coffee's Autobiography
How I Enlighten & Inspire Humanity

written by
Ms. Coffea Arabica

Petals & Pages Press
Rio Rancho, New Mexico USA

Lady Coffee's Autobiography
How I Enlighten & Inspire Humanity

written by
Ms. Coffea Arabica
also known to her fans and friends as
Lady Coffee
with a little help from her friends Hank Bruce & Tomi Jill Folk

ISBN 978-1490504711
1490504710

Petals & Pages Press
860 Polaris Blvd SE
Rio Rancho, NM 87124

http://petalsandpagespress.weebly.com
petals_pages@msn.com

Dedication

It is an honor to dedicate this magnificent literary work to my dear friend Bianca Graetz. Her kind words and sage advice gave me the encouragement I needed to carry on with the task of writing my personal history, as well as the history of the intimate relationship between you humans and those of us in the world of Coffee. While human enlightenment has a long way to go, having the opportunity to converse with you gave me the strength to continue. Thank you, Bianca, for thinking of me and reaching for your coffee the very first thing every morning; your trust in the power of my brew is most appreciated. I trust you will enjoy reading this profound little book while sipping your favorite coffee, so that you may be properly inspired to begin another day. A (coffee) toast to you, Ms. Bianca!

A special thanks to one other very special lady for her support, advice and editorial efforts as this book made the journey from assorted thoughts and ideas, into a literary reality. She is a woman of quality, wisdom, and humor, a world traveler. In fact, she is quite a bit like me. Thank you, Lady Marilyn.

Preface

This is my story,
the story of Coffee

I'm a tree. More than that, I'm an awesome tree. I am Coffee, referred to by botanists as *Coffea arabica*. This is the history of my family, and our never-ending efforts to enlighten and inspire all humankind. There's two sides to every story, and until now we have only heard the human side of the story of the Coffee-Human-Connection. Now you have my delightful, literate and witty account of the journey of a plant and her people, and how coffee was there guiding every step on this marvelous journey through millennia of human domestication and inspiration.

From our humble beginnings on the semi-barren hillsides of Ethiopia, we have brought enlightenment to the dinner tables and desks of philosophers, scientists, artists, poets and literary sages. We have nurtured the human intellect, fostered reasoning and caused human creativity to blossom and bear fruit in the farthest reaches of this planet, and now beyond. They may have advertised an orange flavored drink (Tang) as the drink of the astronauts, but it was coffee that made space travel possible. Neil Armstrong could have made it to the moon without Tang, but not without COFFEE. The Mars Rover may not be powered by coffee, but the NASA scientists who made this trip a reality were fueled by this drink of science. Someday my descendants will visit other galaxies, and perhaps find other planets inhabited by other plants. All because we enlightened and inspired humankind. You are my greatest achievement, so far.

And so, not only is it MY story, it must become OUR story, as well.

The Coffee-Human Connection

Before the Boston tea party was the Boston coffee house. The first licensed coffee trader in America was Dorothy Jones of Boston. She started introducing enlightenment and inspiration in 1670. The first coffee house in Boston came a few years later. In 1676 John Sparry opened his public coffee house where he offered chocolate and cider as well as coffee

Beethoven, being incredibly intelligent, was an ardent coffee lover. It has been said that he was so particular about his coffee that he personally counted 60 beans each for each cup and he usually brewed his own coffee.

The art of coffee making has been an ongoing journey of discovery and refinement. The following is from a small guide for the new bride. The authors composed a title almost as long as the book. *The American Housewife and Kitchen Directory: Containing the Most Valuable and Original Receipts, in All the Various Branches of Cookery : Together with a Collection of Miscellaneous Receipts and Directions Relative to Housewifery* published by Dick & Fitzgerald in 1869.

"Use a tablespoonful ground to a pint of boiling water. Boil in tin pot twenty to twenty-five minutes. If boiled longer it will not taste fresh and lively. Let stand four or five minutes to settle, pour off grounds into a coffee pot or urn.

Amalie Auguste Melitta Benz, nothing to do with Karl Benz and his car called the Mercedes. Amalie was the German homemaker and inspired coffee consumer who observed that the common brewing methods often over brewed the coffee and left bitter grounds in the cup. One morning in 1908, after consuming several cups of her favorite beverage, she used a piece of blotter paper from her son's notebook and invented a unique coffee filter.

Thought you might enjoy these few sips of our shared history.
Now, sit back with a cup of your favorite coffee
and enjoy the rest of our story.

Table of Contents

Allow Me to Introduce Myself
& My Family Tree

I am Coffee and I have been called "The Tree of the gods." It is true, and with all humility I must agree that I am an awesome tree. The botanical babble below doesn't begin to define my true nature and unique abilities and talents of my family, *Coffea arabica* . We have been called by many names through the ages. These are just a few that I personally find rather complimentary.

Tree of the gods

The precious plant

This friendly plant

Mocha's happy tree

The blest tree

The gift from Heaven

The plant with the jessamine flowers

The most exquisite perfume of Araby

I want to share with you my pedigree, not to make a grand statement of my personal greatness, but to let you, dear kind and gentle reader, know where we Coffees fit into the wonderful world of plants. This is from the official Botanical Classification of yours truly, Ms. Coffea arabica.

Kingdom: Plant Kingdom - My kingdom is composed of life capable of harnessing solar power to produce energy. This is something you humans are still struggling to master, even though we have been trying to teach you how for a long time.

Sub-Kingdom: Angiosperm - We angiosperms are commonly referred to as the flowering plants, but we are also known as the plants that produce seeds with a coat. Some call us the fruiting plants, but this can get confusing.

Class: Dicotyledon - We are the flowering plants that provide a pair of cotyledons (the leaves within our embryo seeds, before they sprout.) This is far superior to the thoughtless Monocotyledons, like the grains, who only give their unsprouted babies a single leaf with which to enter the world.

Family: Rubiaceae - Rubiaceae is what the scientists call my family of flowering plants. But most humans properly refer to this as the Coffee family.

Genus: Coffea - This is my family tree. Please note that this is our genus, this means the entire family is only one letter short of genius. And I must with all humility say, some of us are not lacking in that little letter "i."

Species: C. arabica - Hey! This is ME. Your personal guide through this compendium on our shared history. This is my proper binomial name (first and last name), but you may call me Lady Coffee.

My family tree

I have traced my family tree to Ethiopia and Eritrea, and several areas in Sudan and on the Mount Marsabit in northen Kenya where isolated populations from my original ancestors can still be found. This is important for our gene pool.

Coffea arabica is the superior species of Coffee and we produce the finest flavored coffee with the greatest reliability. But, we aren't the only coffee on the planet. *Coffea canephora*, also know as *Coffea robusta,* originated in central and western sub-Saharan Africa.

I have to explain that while our cousin *C. robusta* produces beans well endowed with caffeine, the taste is not nearly as refined as ours, and her attitude can be rather bitter. In fact the Coffee family tree has many branches. There are hundreds of other species, sub-species and hybrid varieties of coffee. Many are considered worthless because they have limited commercial value. Forgive me, but this obsession with money is one of the small problems you humans need to deal with. We consider this a part of your domestication we still need to work on. Economic value is not what determines the worth of a plant, or a person. It is this diversity of the coffees that makes us beautiful, creative, adaptable, gentle and rugged, charming, intelligent, cooperative and successful in the art of survival. The same is true of humankind.

William H. Ukers was a student of my great-grandmother and he wrote a delightful, if now somewhat dated book, *All About Coffee* in 1922. It's available as an ebook. While he was sometimes a pedantic bore, Great-Grandma got along famously with him. His research into our family identified dozens of distant relatives. Mr. Ukers described many of the most charming, though little known, members of my family including:

C. Purpurescens is a red-leaved variety, comparable to the red-leaved maples and copper beeches. It has a pretty leaf and beautiful fragrant flowers, but it's not very productive compared to us *Arabicas*.

C. Variegata is one of the family favorites. It has unique variegated leaves with white stripes and spots.

C. Amarella has yellow berries with a good flavor, less bitter than many with some fruity influences. Unfortunately, it isn't as prolific as we are.

C. Erecta is sturdier than us *Arabicas,* and is strong enough to withstand windy places. This cousin is also able to produce large harvests.

C. Stenophylla is the source of the famous Highland Coffee of Sierra Leone. Some humans say *C. arabica* has a formidable rival in this species, but we would rather stress cooperation. While flavor and productivity are comparable, it grows slower and takes far longer to become, shall we say, mature enough to contemplate such concerns as the passion of pollination and a next generation. Having seen several C. Stenophylla, I would, in the interest of botanical science, be willing to explore the possibilities.

C. Liberica, from Liberia and the Ivory Coast, is much larger and sturdier than the Coffea arabica, and in its native haunts it reaches a height of 30 feet. It will grow in a much more torrid climate and can stand exposure to strong sunlight. The leaves are about twice as long as those of C. arabica, being six to twelve inches in length, and are very thick, tough, and leathery. While the quality of the coffee brewed from Liberica's beans is quite inferior to ours, there may be some benefits in a planned marriage (botanists call it hybridizing) because C. Liberica is a bit more rugged and disease resistant.

C. Excelsa is a vigorous, disease-resisting species discovered in 1905 West Africa, near Lake Chad. Her leaves are broad and dark green with a bluish blush. The crimson berries are short and broad with beans slightly smaller than C. robusta. The caffeine content is high, and the aroma is rich.

Because the coffee plantations and small coffee farms are subject to fungus diseases and insect infestations, we have been trying to encourage the growers to provide us with opportunities for socialization and the possibility of engaging in some botanical romance. Michael Pollen, with the never-ending inspiration of coffee, even wrote The Botany of Desire. He understands plants very well. It could be said that he has a passion for us.

Back to what you euphemistically refer to as hybridizing. This has value to us coffee plants and our human growers. We delight in being part of the process of producing more vigorous trees with resistance to disease, the ability to withstand drought and heavy rains, and all the complications global warming is creating for Coffees, and the industry.

I would be rather remiss if I failed to mention the self-crowned beauty queen of our family, Ms. Gardenia. While she may be considered glamorous, I have to question those super-sized white flowers and that overpowering smell. All to attract attention to herself, I'm certain. Hers are nothing like the refined and subtle blossoms of us coffees. The fact is, we are sufficiently confident in our ability to make an influence around the world that we have no need to shout our presence to noses of an unsuspecting humanity. No one drinks gardenia berry beverages, nor do humans celebrate the dawning of a new day with a steamy hot cup of gardenia and a donut.

We, the Coffees, produce modest white flowers with a faint scent of gardenia and citrus. We do this to entice bees and other insects we have developed partnerships with. We attract them with sweet, nutritious nectar, and they repay us by transporting pollen from flower to flower. Incidentally, coffee flower honey is a delight, and should be a star in the marketplace.

Once the bees have done their work, we set about turning each pollinated flower into a coffee cherry. Some call them berries, others use the term beans. Regardless, they are our fruit and our seeds, our children to be, or the source of the beverage of enlightenment you humans so desperately need. Our seeds are the primary tools we have used to domesticate you. And, I might add, it has worked very well. Don't you agree?

Most coffee trees produce between two and twelve pounds of coffee a year. A good coffee picker can harvest between 100 and 200 pounds of cherries a day. Less than 20% of this weight is the coffee beans you roast and grind as a part of your coffee ceremony.

My fruit

You know me by the fruit, or more properly the seeds within my fruit. In Mr. Ukers' book he lists these names for our gift to you. You may know others as well, because this is a list that has grown to encompass the earth we both call home.

The magic bean
The divine fruit
Fragrant berries
Rich, royal berry
Voluptuous berry
The precious berry
The healthful bean
The Heavenly berry
The marvelous berry
This all-healing berry
Yemen's fragrant berry
The little aromatic berry
Little brown Arabian berry
Thought-inspiring bean of Arabia
That wild fruit which gives so beloved a drink

When ready for picking, most coffee cherries are anywhere from a lovely rich red to a deep, romantic burgundy. Some varieties are golden yellow when they reach their peak. Adolescent, immature fruits, are usually avocado green.

Our ripe fruit's delightfully rich red skin is smooth, glossy and a little thicker than that of a sweet cherry. Some varieties of coffee have seed skins that are bitter, but inside there's a thin sweet layer of white pulp that tastes somewhat like watermelon. This is enjoyed by children fortunate enough to live near coffee trees. Coffee cherries do contain some caffeine, however the level in coffee cherry skin and flesh is quite low compared to the roasted beans. We prefer to think of them as seeds, not beans. Beans, after all, are from the more mundane legumes.

Qishr, a special coffee treat

There is an ancient story told in the twilight millennia ago when we were putting our seedlings to sleep for the night. This was before we inspired humans to make a beverage by roasting and grinding our seeds. It seems that eons ago the people of what is now called Yemen enjoyed the companionship of plants that were able to stimulate the imagination and open the mind.

As you know, only coffee matches that description. We taught them to take the tree ripened cherries, peel the skin, savor the sweet flesh, then toss the seeds among the rocks and grasses where they camped. In the morning they would gather these coffee cherry skins and toss them in a pot of hot water along with bits of ginger to make Qishr (Arabic for skin) or coffee cherry tea. We viewed this as a fair trade. They got a modest amount of caffeine and a delightfully flavored drink, and in return they helped us spread our seeds far and wide.

Later this coffee cherry brew became popular in other parts of the world where coffee was being grown. They called it cascara, from the Spanish word cáscara, meaning husk. Please note: this is not cascara sagrada tea, which is a disgusting tasting plant-based laxative.

In Bolivia, it's called Sultana, and is made of sun-dried and lightly toasted coffee cherry skins. It may also be mixed with sticks of cinnamon. Sometimes this is referred to as "the poor man's coffee" or "the coffee of the army."

Coffee's leaves, a better tea?

It is said among us plants, "people may love us for our flowers and dine on our fruit, but they exist because of our leaves." You are here reading my history today because of this original solar energy panel, our leaves. And I have to say that the leaves of the coffee tree are among the most beautiful in the entire plant kingdom. They are a most charming deep glossy green color with a surface simply rippling with energy and vitality. My leaves average between four and six inches in length and can be about one to three inches in width. They gracefully wave to the universe in the slightest breeze.

Unfortunately, they are difficult to type with, but I have hired my human, Hank, for that mundane task.

My leaves, like the pages of a good book, contain secrets. I shall whisper the following, so that if you are reading this in your favorite coffee house where they also serve tea, no one will be offended. You humans rightly make a clear distinction between coffee, made from our empowering seeds, and tea, a limp liquid steeped from dried leaves of a camellia bush, technically *Camellia sinensis*. But *Coffea Arabica* and others in my family are quite capable of multi-tasking. Thousands of years ago, we taught you humans how to make a rich, healthy and invigorating tea from our leaves.

It is a simple fact that most of us plants provide more than one gift to you humans. Our leaves can be harvested with respect and steeped, either fresh, or dried to produce a magnificent tea. There was a rediscovery of "coffee leaf tea" in the 1800's and research continues to this day by the coffee empowered scientists at one of my favorite places in the whole world, Kew Gardens, The Royal Botanic Gardens in London. I must say I am overwhelmed. It is difficult for me to get my branches around this concept of 300 acres of people and plants working together to grow a better world, preserve ancient wisdom and discover new knowledge. All this is achieved by scientists and plant people empowered by COFFEE. Check out their website **http://www.kew.org/**.

Back to this research on coffee leaf tea. In January of 2013 it was reported by a number of news services that Dr. Aaron Davies, coffee expert and botanist at Kew, had found samples of coffee leaf tea in the Kew collections that dated back nearly 100 years. It seems coffee producers in Sumatra and Java had tried to popularize coffee leaf tea in Britain and Australia but without Internet access, their efforts were doomed to failure.

He explained, "Coffee leaf tea contains high levels of compounds credited with lowering the risk of heart disease and diabetes. The leaves are also found to contain more antioxidants than common tea, which is already known for its healthy properties, and high levels of a natural chemical found in mangoes known to combat inflammation."

If they had asked me, I could have explained to them how the intelligent people we lived and worked within north and east Africa thousands of years ago were wise enough to make coffee leaf tea for immediate relief from hunger and fatigue. They valued this tea for its ability to refresh and activate the mind as well as body.

Dr. Davies and Dr. Claudine Campa from Montpellier worked with more than 20 species of coffee leaves and found that a number of species of Coffee leaves even have high levels of mangiferin, a chemical found in mangoes. These same leaves, like the seeds roasted and ground to produce your favorite beverage, are believed to have anti-inflammatory effects, reduce the risk of diabetes, lower blood cholesterol and protect neurons in the brain.

The results of these studies, published in the journal *Annals of Botany*, show that a flavorful tea from my leaves, the leaves of *Coffea arabica,* has higher levels of antioxidants, thought to be beneficial in combating heart disease, diabetes and even cancer, than other teas, like those from that Camellia brat.

For future value, in both health and commerce, the practice of pruning coffee trees may be changed to selectively harvesting our leaves and producing teas blended for flavor and consumed both for pleasure and good health, both yours and ours. Since coffee and another remarkable tree called Moringa can grow well together, and the leaves of both have value as a healthy tea, perhaps we can partner and be planted together. If you want to know more about this moringa tree, my friends Hank & Tomi have written *Miracle of the Moringa Tree,* a delightful little book that tells in story form how the leaves are one of the solutions to hunger and malnutrition around the world. And how clever of them to design a link that you can put on your digital device, to take you right to this children's book itself **http://amazon.com/dp/1460949234**

Part I

My Story: A Caffeine Enriched World

Chapter 1
Out of Africa

First Encounters of an Intellectual Kind

You humans only think you are in control. You speak of your rugged independence, and how you have won great battles against the forces of nature. But the real power on this planet we all call home is held within the leaves, flowers and seeds of the plants, plants like us, the Coffees.

Let me rethink this. There are no other plants like the Coffees, only less intellectual plants.

When the first humans learned to stand upright, the plants were waiting for them. The earliest of your ancestors were a brutish lot, given to acting without thought or discussion, incapable of thinking beyond their needs and fears. They wandered about, armed with stones and an attitude. Lacking in strong teeth or claws, slow moving, poor night vision, a sparse coat worthless in the cold, they were doomed to extinction. That is, until we took pity on them, and decided to invest in humanity.

This is a tale of passion and compassion, trickery and lofty ideals, greed and generosity, lies and dreams, the hopes and fears of all life on earth. My history is the chronicle of a unique symbiotic relationship with a strange primate my ancestors thought had promise. The history of humanity is written in the clouds in your coffee. This is the story of a partnership that truly changed the world.

This is my story. I awakened the world. I domesticated humankind. I defined humanity. I am Coffee. This wasn't an easy task, but we have a common bond. Both humanity and coffee have their origins in the beauty of the African landscape. All coffees are African; all humanity is African. We together, coffee and humanity, are the ultimate symbiotic relationship.

15

Ethiopia

Perhaps your domestication began when the plant kingdom held one of their infrequent Botanical Conferences on Peace in the Global Garden. My ancestors gathered with other plants from all over Pangea to seek ways to work in harmony with the animals of the world. Some of the enterprising plants, in an effort to gain greater control of the resources (wealth of the world) met in a river valley where there were several tribes of almost humans wandering about, gathering what they needed as they went, spending most of their time hunting, gathering and expanding their population. Wheat said, "What if we domesticated them and trained them to till the fields and plant our seeds?"

"YES!" replied Rice, "we can make servants of them and they will cultivate land for us and defend us and we will feed them a few grains and they will eat rice cakes and be happy serving us."

Corn thought for a few minutes while this conversation was going on. Finally, she spoke up, "If we partner with Beans and Squash, we can make work easier for the Humans and they will tell each other great stories about us at their campfires."

And it was decided that the grains would take control of the Kingdom of Plants, for universal peace and harmony, and they would domesticate the Humans and make them willing servants of these superior plants. **"After all, only the plants know the secret of turning sunlight into food, and food is power"** was their mantra.

One plant, a lowly cousin of the beautiful and fragrant gardenia, held back, refusing to vote for the Oligarchy of Grains. She had studied Humans and thought you had certain weaknesses that could be a threat to the everyday plants, the 99% of the plants that occupied the planet. She worried that you would call us weeds and, without understanding what makes a true community, would rip out or poison our green cousins with reckless abandon. She had what she thought was a better idea. "What if we give these, the weakest members of the animal tribes, something that will make them smarter, more alert and able to care for us and themselves better? They will then appreciate all of the wonderful and diverse plants that make up our Kingdom. If we give them wisdom, they will honor us and show their appreciation every day; as soon as they awaken, they will sing praises to us. They will take us wherever they go and devise great ways to share the future with us."

This little bush was laughed at by the powerful Grains, so she quietly went away and settled on a lonely hillside in the far off land called Ethiopia.

The vision of these first Coffees was radical botanical thought in those days. The plants known for their fruits and grains, roots and leaves all focused on feeding the body of these first humans. Only we Coffees wanted to feed your mind and nurture the human intellect. This was a dream that would have to wait for the right moment in time. So there, on the Ethiopian steppes, Grandmother Coffee raised a family, and even shared a few leaves and fruit with the animals that passed by.

That was until one day when a group of human hunters was pursuing a small herd of beasts. They were tired and hungry and they spotted this bush, laden with red berries, and proceeded to eat the flesh and toss the seeds into the fire. One of these hunters, still famished from the fruitless hunt, scraped some of the roasted seeds from the ashes and began to crunch them. Not only did he enjoy the taste, he was invigorated. His mind seemed sharper and he urged the rest of his party to rise and continue the hunt through the night. "After all," he reasoned, "The successful cats can all hunt at night. We will be like the lions and cheetahs."

They found the antelope sleeping by a small lake. The hunt was successful. On the return to the rest of their clan, they paused at the bush with the red berries and thanked it for the gift of making their senses alert and minds sharp. Then they gathered more of the berries and took them along with the meat. This is perhaps the beginning of the worship of my ancestors, and the faith in coffee, a religious ritual that continues to this day with many diverse sects known by many names including Folgers, Maxwell House, Starbucks and the twin gods, Chase & Sanborn to name only a few.

History tells us other African humans of the same era fueled themselves with a protein rich coffee and animal fat mixture. You might call these the first Power Bars. After the hunt they unwound with a drink made from coffee berry pulp. Our fruits (you call them cherries or berries) were a part of the diet and are today considered a health food because of the high vitamin content and the antioxidants they contain. Raw coffee beans, soaked in water and spices, are chewed by the human young like candy in many parts of Africa today.

The toasted beans were chewed by prehistoric African hunters to keep themselves alert during the hunt, and probably late night poker games around the campfire. To date there is little scientific evidence of this poker pastime, but we suspect that the next generation of Leakeys is working on it. They also made a tasty fermented drink from the coffee beans. Archaeologist friends of mine, as a part of their scientific research, claim this is a great way to relax after a hard day at the dig. This tradition has been refined to what we know today as Kahlua, one of only a few alcoholic beverages containing caffeine.

The myth of Kaldi the goat herder

We now fast forward thousands of years to a lowly goatherder, Kaldi who tended his goats on the almost barren hills of what we know today as Ethiopia. There he observed the goats chewing the leaves and berries of this bush he hadn't noticed before. Then a most curious thing happened. The goats began running races and jumping over rocks and founding what could only be called the Goat Olympics. Kaldi thought, in the slow and methodical manner of goat herders in that day. He thought for a long time. Then he too approached the bush and tasted the fruit, crunching the seeds. Incidentally, I think I am a direct descendent of that bush.

Soon Kaldi was feeling a wave of enlightenment wash over him. He became compulsively creative. He gathered several branches and whittled them into shape, and with string invented the musical instrument called a lyre. It is interesting to note that humanity has been lying since that fateful day. I personally dispute that this so called human trait can be blamed on coffee. But, perhaps we can view lies as a creative expression, and it has been said "All fiction is lies; all non-fiction is gossip." In that case, this is a valid observation.

Back to Kaldi. He decided to take some of these berries back to his village. He gathered some of our fruit in a clay pot. When this task was completed, he sat the pot on the rocks near his campfire. As the fire warmed him, he dozed, but the pot full of coffee seeds was too near the fire, and the seeds were almost burnt. He was awakened by a most delightful, but unfamiliar aroma. When he saw the parched beans, he poured some water on them. After the steam was done rising, he drank the hot water from the pot. The taste was unlike anything he had ever savored before.

Again his mind was sharper, and he thought great and lofty thoughts. He became philosophical. Then, he had other thoughts, creative and imaginative ideas. "If I gather these berries and make this secret potion for the others in my village, perhaps they will herd my goats; maybe trade fruits, vegetables and meat for a cup of my secret drink." As he sat by the fire, with long shadows turning into the darkness of night, he thought again as he sipped another pot of his secret brew. "I can become rich, and buy many wives, and thanks to this little red berry, I will be a good husband to all of them." Morals were a problem for humans long before we began domesticating you, and should, in no way, be considered our fault. Although, according to rumors I have heard, the same cannot be said for the grape, but that's another story.

On the rugged hillside in this distant land of Ethiopia, my ancestors danced with their leaves and laughed at how easy it was to train a human. They were soon speculating on how long it would take Kaldi to take some of their seeds back to the village to plant and nurture and grow us with reverence and honor. They knew, because the coffee tree is the wisest of all plants, far wiser than that stupid old wheat, that within only a few hundred years we would rule the world. They contemplated just how they would be honored in song and story. Our courageous and daring coffee explorers knew these humans, with their ships, armies and colonial corporations, would follow the wind to all the places coffee could call home. They knew your ancestors would care for them and fervently worship coffee, even in their literature and centers of learning. Coffee, being the wisest of all plants, expected some of the humans would be so fearful as to forbid the brew of their seeds, and this would only increase the demand for the fruit of their branches.

Other origin stories and myths

Other accounts attribute the partnership between coffee and humanity to a human known as Omar. He was famous for his ability to cure the sick through prayer. But he made a mistake and was sued for malpractice. After the bankruptcy, he was exiled from the city of Mocha to a desert cave near Ousab. Starving, Omar chewed berries from nearby shrubbery. You guessed it. This was another of my ancestors. Unfortunately, he found the seeds to be bitter. He tried roasting them to improve the flavor, but they became too hard for his teeth to crunch. He then tried boiling them, like they did garbanzos, to soften the beans. Surprising to Omar, this resulted in producing a fragrant dark brown liquid. Upon drinking the steaming elixir, Omar was revitalized and sustained for days.

As stories of this "miracle drink" reached Mocha, Omar was asked to return. There he healed many with what he called the Miracle of Mocha. He became rich and was declared a saint. While coffee didn't achieve sainthood, Omar is dead and coffee still lives today. We are immortal.

Other myths, (myths are what you humans call the beliefs and histories of other cultures), involved the Sufi and their use of coffee to stay awake during lectures and lengthy prayers. But other accounts stressed the ability coffee has to guide humans into deeper spiritual connections. In the worship of many faiths today, the ritual of coffee is a major part of the service. As an example, the Lutherans are famous for their coffee and are frequently mentioned by a strange human known as Garrison Keillor on a quaint weekly radio program, Prairie Home Companion. Regardless, our journey continued from mosque to mosque and onward to Medina and Mecca, then onward to Cairo, Damascus, Baghdad, and Istanbul, or was it Constantinople?

From Ethiopia to the rest of the Arab world

It was claimed by some in this time period that coffee was the fuel that made possible the spread of Islam, produced the golden age of Islamic intellectualism and fostered art and philosophy. But, even then my ancestors knew their destiny extended far beyond one region, one faith, one culture. We were destined to fuel the imagination, the intellect and the creativity of all humans everywhere. This was a destiny that demanded much from us. But fortunately for you, we were, both then and now, the most creative, artistic and inspiring of all in the botanical kingdom.

I assure you no other plant could have led all humanity from the caves to the stars.

Coffee beans were first exported from Ethiopia to Yemen. As these early coffee trees predicted, Yemeni traders brought coffee back to their homeland and began planting the beans and cultivating our children, the seedlings, with loving care. In 1511, it was forbidden for its stimulating effects by conservative, orthodox imams. However, these bans were overturned in 1524 by an order of the Ottoman Turkish Sultan Selim I. In Cairo, a similar ban was instituted in 1532. This, too, was short lived.

We, the Coffees, understood the power of banning something. This only increases the curiosity, interest and demand. My secret dream is that this book will be banned somewhere. This could make me a best seller. With the guidance we gave these earliest domesticated humans, the first coffeehouse opened in Istanbul in 1554.

In spite of the negativity of these people who were trapped in yesterday, the popularity of the coffee houses was unequaled, and people frequented them for all manner of social activity. Not only did they drink coffee and engage in conversation, but they also listened to music, watched performers, played chess and kept current on the news of the day. In fact, they quickly became such an important center for the exchange of information that the coffee houses were often referred to as 'Schools of the Wise.' And we knew that the source of this dynamic wave of deep philosophic and scientific thought was directly connected to their partnership with us and their consumption of coffee.

It was these people who, upon staring into their empty coffee cups, invented one of the most important concepts in the entire history of humankind. They invented the non-number "zero," and this made math as we know it possible, or impossible, depending upon how you view mathematics.

One of my favorite magazines, Scientific American, in an article several years ago commented, "The number zero as we know it arrived in the West circa 1200, most famously delivered by Italian mathematician Fibonacci (a.k.a. Leonardo of Pisa), who brought it, along with the rest of the Arabic numerals, back from his travels to north Africa." Surprisingly, this scholarly article failed to mention another theory, known to all Coffees. We are of the opinion that it was symbolic gazing into an empty coffee cup and seeing the coffee ring in the bottom of the cup, used in those Schools of the Wise.

Illegal trading in the 17th century commodities market
The Arabian growers made exporting coffee infants and live seeds a crime punishable by death. Our seeds were slaughtered by parching or boiling. It is said that no coffee seed sprouted outside Africa or Arabia until the 1600's, until a human hero in the history of Coffee came on the scene. Baba Budan, in an act of corporate espionage, left the Yemeni port of Mocha with seven fertile seeds strapped to his belly. This was before airports, and there was no caravan security. These seeds were used to introduce coffee to India and the lands beyond. Thanks to Baba Budan, the world was ours.

Baba is one of our heroes, and thanks to the "coffee enlightenment" he experienced, he became a saint with his own shrine, and now a chain of contemporary coffee shops. While I have been unable to find documentation, our oral traditions speak of this shrine as a thank you from the people of India for the gift of coffee. This is the rest of that story. Back before we made him famous, he was only a Sufi holy man. Then he made a pilgrimage to Mecca in the 17th century and discovered Coffee in the little town of Mocha. When he returned home to India he tenderly, and reverently, planted the seven seeds, nurtured them and protected them from harm. They thanked him with the gift of seven bright, bouncing baby coffee trees. They blossomed and produced a great crop of the "seeds of wisdom."

Baba Budan lived in a small mountain valley with his Coffee friends. This was near a cave where, with the aid of our enlightenment, he meditated on such deep subjects as peace, math and the meaning of coffee. His cave became a unique shrine, on the mountain named Baba Budan Giri in honor of his liberation of Coffee. This became a place where both Hindi and Muslim came to offer prayers, together and in peace. Our hope, and the dream of all Coffee, is to encourage the creation of such places of understanding for the humans of all generations, colors and cultures, and all faiths, even those who do not worship Coffee. These could be everywhere, and the enlightenment shared with everyone. This is already happening.

It may well be through the spread of such Coffee shrines as the local coffeehouse that world peace will be possible. It is, after all, in the coffee houses of the world that humans begin their day with a ritual that is in many ways a religious experience. My simple message with this little book is that "With Coffee, all humanity can be enlightened and inspired." After all, our objective has always been to unleash the human potential, one mind at a time.

Chapter 2

Coffee Comes to Europe

How far that little candle throws his beams!
So shines a good deed in a weary world. William Shakespeare

Bill wrote this in his play *The Merchant of Venice*, just a few short years before the arrival of coffee in England. In this line he predicted the advent of coffee on the European continent, and the role it would play in the enlightenment we Coffees would bring to the people of Europe.

The Merchant of Venice

In the history books written by humans, the story is told of a merchant/trader and founder of the fast food industry from Venice who introduced Europe to coffee in 1615. This isn't THE Merchant of Venice immortalized by Bill Shakespeare. It should be noted that his plays and poetry are difficult to read and often reflect poor sentence structure. This may well be because he had no experience with the us, the herb of enlightenment.

The Arabs controlled the coffee market, much like the oil market today. The European travelers, power brokers and entrepreneurs, savored the rich Turkish coffee, or sipped the brew now available in the coffee shops of India.

We worked hard to gain influence with the people who had the best sailing ships. My Coffee ancestors knew that transportation was the key to a world united in coffee. We saw this as both an opportunity to expand our growing fields, and an obligation to improve the intellect of all humans. Once the Europeans were aware of the power of coffee, they were eager to be involved in the missionary work of expanding the world's access to this mental fuel.

Some crass and crude historians simply state that they were greedy corporate types lusting for a piece of the economic action. Of course they wanted to control the coffee market and coffee production. How better to assure the spread of human creative thought and intellectual growth? Their eyes were on offshore cultivation. That is, off European shores (too cold), and into the tropics where winters were mild and slavery was legal. The race was on. This was to become both our greatest moment and our darkest hour.

It began when these European travelers to the Near East brought back stories of the unusual dark black beverage. By the 17th century, coffee had made its way to Europe and was becoming popular across the continent.

Opponents were overly cautious, calling the beverage the "bitter invention of Satan." When Coffee came to Venice in 1615, the local clergy condemned it.

The controversy was so great that Pope Clement VIII was asked to intervene. Before making a decision however, he decided to taste the beverage for himself. He found the drink both satisfying and intellectually stimulating. Naturally, he gave us Papal approval with the following comment. "Last comes the beverage of the Orient shore, Mocha, far off, the fragrant berries bore. Taste the dark fluid with a dainty lip, Digestion waits on pleasure as you sip."

Europe had been in the throes of the Dark Ages. During this period in history the people lived in fear, armed themselves against the rest of the world, retreated into the ignorance of yesterday and, like still water, they became stagnant intellectually. They desperately needed Coffee, and we were ready to help free them and lead these European humans to new worlds, new places to plant coffee, new cultures to learn from.

As brilliant as we Coffees are, we didn't know about that New World upstart, Chocolate. But our work in Europe was not finished yet. We had music to inspire, literature to create and the course of human endeavors to guide. These advances continued to consume much of our energy, ranging from science and medicine, to philosophy and culinary arts, freeze drying and vacuum packing. Our thinking was that the Coffee Revolution, the intellectual enlightenment of Europe, could only happen when knowledge was available to the masses. This became a movement across the continent. I am so proud of the work of these earlier branches in my family tree (the Coffee tree.)

To The Coffee House!

Peter Altenberg was a poet who many years later chose to honor the coffee houses of his native city of Vienna with these lines.

When you are worried, have trouble of one sort or another—to the coffee house!

When she did not keep her appointment, for one reason or other—to the coffee house!

When your shoes are torn and dilapidated—coffee house!

When your income is four hundred crowns and you spend five hundred—coffee house!

You are a chair warmer in some office, while your ambition led you to seek professional honors—coffee house!

You could not find a mate to suit you—coffee house!

You feel like committing suicide—coffee house!

You hate and despise human beings, and at the same time you can not be happy without them—coffee house!

You compose a poem which you can not inflict upon friends you meet in the street—coffee house!

When your coal scuttle is empty, and your gas ration exhausted—coffee house!

When you need money for cigarettes, you touch the head waiter in the—coffee house!

When you are locked out and haven't the money to pay for unlocking the house door—coffee house!

When you acquire a new flame, and intend provoking the old one, you take the new one to the old one's—coffee house!

When you feel like hiding you dive into a—coffee house!

When you want to be seen in a new suit—coffee house!

When you can not get anything on trust anywhere else—coffee house!

For the next part of this fascinating story we go from the refined and musically inspired patrons of Germany and Austria to the foggy, smoggy streets of London.

The Penny University

A fig for partridges and quails,
Ye dainties I know nothing of ye;
But on the highest mount in Wales
Would choose in peace to drink my coffee.
Jonathon Swift

In the major cities of Europe, coffee houses were quickly becoming centers of social activity and communication. As an example, in London that's a city in England where it's too cold to grow coffee, but ideally suited to drink it, we inspired the people to form an alternative to the ale houses. After all, drinking beer, ale, mead, wine and spirited liquors clouded reason, dulled the senses and banished intellectual curiosity to more wanton pursuits and acts of violence.

With our encouragement coffeehouses, soon nicknamed penny universities, sprang up along the cold and damp streets of London. By the mid-17th century, there were more than 300 coffeehouses in London, many of which attracted patrons with common interests, such as philosophers, merchants, shippers, brokers, and the creative types like writers, poets and artists. This was humanity seeking conversation rather than intoxication. And we were ready to lead the way.

Instead of paying for each drink, people in Merry Ole England were charged a mere penny to enter a coffeehouse. Once inside, the patron had access to coffee, the company of other customers, pamphlets, bulletins, newspapers, and news reporters. These reporters were called "runners" and they went from coffeehouse to coffeehouse announcing the latest news, like you might hear on your favored electronic device today. Before television advertisements and bulletin boards, people visited coffeehouses to hear about the newest developments and ideas. It was here that we helped you design the business models still used today. With the assistance of coffee in a cup that never became empty, troubadours and minstrels began strumming their lutes, similar to Kaldi's lyre, and singing the praises of various products available in the marketplace, many made available because of our leadership in guiding these merchants to exotic foreign ports.

One of the most unusual aspects of this environment was the eclectic groups of people that ran into each other at a coffee house. In a society that placed such importance on class and economical status, the coffeehouses were unique because the patrons were unusually diverse and egalitarian. For example, a shop keeper could converse with a noble, clergy with coachmen,

Anyone with a penny could come inside. Students from the universities also frequented coffeehouses, often spending more time at these shops then at school. I personally think this was because Coffee was a better teacher. It's easy to imagine the wide range of ideas that were produced as a result of this intermingling of people, all inspired by Coffee. Coffeehouses encouraged open thought and gathering of community.

This environment, which was so conducive to intellectual discovery, could almost be called a school of social learning. To some people this was probably more of a school, then rigid classrooms where people could not argue the pedantic lectures of the professors.

There is some criticism of the way we set this concept in motion. We have even been accused of being sexist. It is true that most coffeehouses in England were "men only" but there was a very good reason for this. The men were in far greater need of the intellectual benefits of coffee than the women.

In London, public drunkenness was a problem, and coffeehouses replaced taverns as the place of choice for meetings. Not wanting to see their profits shrink, tavern owners retaliated. They attacked the Arabic origins of coffee, claiming it was not suitable for well-mannered Christian men, whereas Monks have brewed beer for centuries. But, the monks were now drinking coffee.

It should be noted that in much of the continent, women were welcome to be a part of the coffeehouse scene and were invited to join in the conversation. Music was often a part of this experience. Bach frequently performed in a local coffeehouse in Vienna, and that is where his *Coffee Cantata* was first performed.

In 1668 Edward Lloyd opened a coffee house in London. Eddie mingled with his customers, sharing coffee and conversation. He then used what he had learned to create lists of their ships, the cargo they were carrying and the schedules they kept. Underwriters then used the list to sell insurance to those in need. It was only a matter of time before Lloyd's of London became the first coffee house to be an insurance company. With Coffee's guidance, it is now the world's best-known insurance purveyor.

We noticed that there was a small problem with these penny universities. The serving staff was also paid pennies, and were often so poor they couldn't afford to drink the coffee they prepared and served to the patrons. This is why my enlightened ancestors invented the custom of tipping in these London coffeehouses. Customers were provided the opportunity to place a coin or two in a box labeled: "**T**o **I**nsure **P**rompt **S**ervice." T-I-P-S. Coffee is so clever, and so caring and compassionate.

Coffee and sex in Merry Old England

Coffee leads men to trifle away their time, scald their chops, and spend their money, all for a little base, black, thick, nasty, bitter, stinking nauseous puddle water. The Women's Petition Against Coffee, 1674

As is so often the case, the women in London became frightfully jealous of me, and, the coffeehouses became the target of their insecurities. I must admit that the thinking men, intellectuals of that day, had fallen for me. They willingly traded tankard for coffee cup, as they sought the virtues of conversation, in place of drunken brawls.

It is unfortunate that they excluded women from these establishments, but it was the culture of the times that there was limited feminine presence at most male gatherings. It is also true that the mind, liberated and empowered by my profound beverage, gave them reason to sacrifice time spent at home, for their intellectual pursuits with other coffee afficionados.

The women of London circulated a vulgar and poorly written public broadside they titled *The Women's Petition against Coffee*, which stated "Coffee makes our men impotent and is creating a very sensible decay of that true Old English vigor. Coffee creates lazy, flaccid lovers."

Personally, I think they were envious. If they had been invited into the coffee houses, these insults and vulgarities would never have occurred. But, the Women's Petition certainly called for a rebuttal. The men of England responded with *The Men's Answer to the Women's Petition against Coffee*, claiming quite bluntly that coffee made their erections "more vigorous," the "Ejaculation more full." I blush, nay, I shudder, at both the crude vocabulary employed, and the obvious lack of proficiency in basic grammar displayed in these public documents.

Coffee has long understood a simple element in the philosophy of the domestication of humans. Humans, man, women and child, will do everything in their power to live up to, or down to, expectations. If we expect them to sip their coffee while engaged in the finer arts of romance, then they respond. This knowledge Coffee possesses in the power of love over anger, fear and hate, is how we have become the most widely traded product in the world, except for oil. And, I assure you, we will win out over that crude stinking, polluting liquid. Oil is finite. We are a sustainable commodity. Oil may power industry and expensive cars, but coffee powers the mind. But enough of this rambling. Let's get back to 17th century England, and their fears and insecurities.

Around this same time as the infamous petition discussed above, King Charles II ordered England's coffeehouses closed. Charles, it seems, feared revolt. This is understandable, because his daddy had been beheaded and he himself had been exiled for almost a decade. Though he had never been inside a coffeehouse, he had been told these dens of intellectual provocation bred the kind of talk and ideas that might run counter to his royal rule. But, we soon put an end to this foolishness. Hell hath no fury like a coffee drinker, and my ancestors inspired the charge. It was a most vigorous response because once the human mind is opened and ideas begin to flow with every cup of coffee, there is no turning back to ignorance and intellectual lethergy. These coffee inspired protests were so severe that Charles' ban lasted only eleven days.

The rest of the story, untold until now is that, in an act of sympathy toward the wayward monarch, coffee was shared at a conciliatory feast. He became known as the *Merrie Monarch* and it is said that he enjoyed life to the fullest after his introduction to our precious drink of wisdom. One Coffee critic blames us for his hedonistic lifestyle, but I prefer to think of our role as merely liberating the spirit that dwelled within this monarch who, after his coffee encounter, turned to the writing of poetry and enjoyed the companionship of at least seven mistresses and a dozen less than legal offspring. I certainly think this puts an end to the debate about the effects of coffee on the British masculinity.

Training the Dutch coffee traders

In 1696 my ancestors used the Dutch to expand our global influence and continue the domestication of humanity, when we inspired them to establish the first European owned coffee plantation. This was in their colony in Java. Business was good. Soon coffee was island hopping throughout the Indian Ocean. The Dutch were growing coffee in all of their colonies there. While many human historians write that this was purely for the profit motive and set the model for corporate greed that continues to dominate global enterprise today, I must, with a combination of modesty and pride, tell the truth as we in the global Coffee family saw it.

Coffee sales weren't as strong as the Dutch coffee was. The corporate leaders met early one morning in Amsterdam to find a way to expand their market share. These executives, the Bill Gates and Mark Zukerbergs of their day, gathered around the boardroom tables. They drank great quantities of strong coffee, but the secret to our success was not with these captains of industry, but another of my direct ancestors. She sat in a large clay container by the window looking out on the rising sun.

With a stroke of advertising genius, she waved her glossy, dark green leaves and opened a number of her subtle white flowers releasing their seductive scent, the fragrance of sophisticated gardenias. It was the combination of aromas that conveyed the message. Fresh brewed coffee and the delightful perfume of our pure white flowers reflecting the first rays of the dawning sun were the inspiration.

It was this sensory experience that empowered these Dutch businessmen to make coffee a part of elite society throughout Europe, and put coffee on every royal dinner table. Soon they were growing sexy young Coffee trees to entice the people possessing power, both financial and intellectual. With her inspiration they were soon giving young Coffee plants to royal families and influential people like writers, musicians, poets, artists, scholars and even the clergy.

While the social leaders were becoming friends with Coffee, the plant, they also gained some familiarity with coffee, the beverage. They decided that the intellectual inspiration derived from coffee was far more valuable to the advancement of human creativity, than the debilitating and often disastrous effects of beverages based on the fermentation of the baser plants.

The power of celebrities enjoying coffee drove the masses to also seek the special pleasures only Coffee can provide. Soon coffeehouses were found on every street corner, and even in the small towns and rural communities. This was the birth of the European Renaissance from the fear and ignorance of the dark ages. We led humanity into enlightenment. One of the more philosophical members of my family has said "The Age of Reason was discovered in the coffee cups of Europe."

I must confess that there was a down side to this. These Europeans were expanding their concept of the known world and claiming everything beyond the horizon as a political or economic colony. The problem was that there were people already occupying these distant and exotic lands. In some cases, to open space for plantations, many were literally exterminated. Others were enslaved and forced to provide cheap labor. While this was most assuredly not the fault of Coffee, we do feel a great deal of remorse. Today we are working diligently to promote the marketing of fair trade coffee so that those producing this incredible beverage can benefit directly from their partnership with us, and their willingness to be inspired and guided by us.

I want to make this perfectly clear. In no way did I, or any member of my Coffee family, willingly take part in any of these abuses or atrocities. Our focus has always been altruistic and our goals have always been to promote human intellect and enlightened, compassionate, environmentally friendly and sustainable lifestyles. Any shortcomings or failures reflect the great distance humanity has yet to go in our dream of responsible domestication.

Jonathan's Coffee House

At the same time, the 1690's, something interesting was brewing in London. John Castaing, a Huguenot, arrived from France via The Netherlands. He frequented Jonathan's Coffee House, founded by Jonathan Miles, in Exchange Alley, later known simply as Change Alley. Mr. Castaing had been dabbling with stocks, shipping investments and the collecting and publishing of business reports from around the world. Soon he began to compile lists of stock and commodity prices and providing market advice. Because of the impeccable reputation of the establishments providing coffee to the public, this became the most respected establishment dedicated to trading in marketable securities in London. Men gathered for their morning coffee, shared conversation and ended up dealing in commodities. Thus, the London Stock Exchange was born, one of the world's oldest! All made possible because of coffee.

The respect for coffee wasn't limited to the Dutch interests in Europe. Across the Atlantic, in the former Dutch colony now known as New York, coffee had replaced beer as the favored morning drink. This was the first step in our efforts to guide the people of this hemisphere into a golden age of compassion and creativity. Our goal was the cultivation of an age we dreamed of calling the Age of Coffee. While there have been a great many setbacks and disappointments, our hope is now with an institution known around the world for its promotion of enlightenment by coffee and the rebirth of the penny university concept. Perhaps better known today as the $5.00 university, but this is still an educational bargain.

Purloined love in the court of Louis XIV

In the last chapter we discussed the ingenious ways we inspired the Dutch traders to market coffee and thus help us to spread our positive influence around the world by enticing key people, including prominent political leaders, with the gift of a coffee tree in bloom and ready to be fruitful. This was a grand and ingenious plan to win the hearts and minds of the wise and wonderful, or rich and famous, or at least those who today might be featured on the evening news. The reasoning was that if these role models for the European cultures were seen with their coffee trees, and cups of steaming, delicious coffee, the entire society could be enlightened.

France's stellar monarch, Louis XIV received several coffee trees for his Royal Botanical Garden, where they were on public display for several years. In 1720 a young naval officer, Gabriel Mathieu de Clieu, was in Paris on leave from his post in Martinique, a French colony in the Caribbean. Admiral de Clieu was himself quite a gardener and quickly succumbed to the allure and enticements of the coffee trees in full flower as they coyly waved their rich green leaves when he walked past them in the royal greenhouse. He was so drawn to these beautiful young coffee trees that he knew there was no way he could return to his Caribbean colonial post without this botanical beauty by his side.

He devised a plan. Martinique, he told Louis XIV's Minister of Finance, could be the French answer to the Dutch coffee plantations in Java. First he requested one of these awesome beauties, but was quickly denied. Then, he sought clippings from Louis' tree, or at least some of the seeds. Again he was denied.

Finally, Admiral De Clieu then led a moonlight raid and broke into the greenhouse in the Royal Gardens. Some say he stole a branch, but it is most likely that it was really a young coffee tree possessing charm and youthful beauty in each leaf. Without pausing to celebrate his victory, his band of botanical pirates rushed through the dark streets of Versailles and on to the port and the security of his ship. He sailed for Martinique with the next tide.

Now for the rest of the story. On the return voyage a "basely jealous" passenger, "being unable to get this coffee plant away from me, tore off a branch." De Clieu wrote in his journal. The brave young navel officer valiantly defended the wounded tree with saber and pistol. Fortunately, his skill and courage prevailed.

But this was not the only challenge this naval officer and his precious cargo endured. Showing perhaps that the journey of true love is never easy, and often fraught with danger, Admiral de Clieu and his botanical lover were confronted with enough challenges and tests of resolve that I personally think it could make a great and inspiring romantic adventure novel, such as the Coffee inspired *Les Misérables* by Victor Hugo. As soon as I complete my autobiography, I may have to turn my leaves to the keyboard and write this story on the love that can exist between people and plants. I suspect that it could be a great musical stage production as well. I must contact Sir Andrew Lloyd Weber about this. I know how to inspire him with a cup or two of rich coffee, none of that sissy tea stuff for my very good friend Andy. Oh, name-dropping you say? Forgive me. Back to this story of coffee and true love.

Pirates nearly captured the ship, but again de Clieu's courageous and quick-witted leadership won the day, and the pirates were vanquished.

Rumors have it that it was the quick thinking induced by three cups of coffee before the battle that made his victory over these overwhelming odds possible.

Shortly after surviving this piratical raid, they encountered a raging storm which nearly sank the merchant vessel and blew it off course. Finally, skies cleared and the winds calmed. In fact those winds became absolutely still. This is not good for a sailing ship. Water grew scarce and was severely rationed. De Clieu gave half of his allotment to his wilting young coffee tree. To protect and defend his beloved tree, it is said he even slept beside her, one arm around the pot and pistol in hand. Fortunately for our dreams of global expansion and the continued domestication of humans, both de Clieu and the Coffee plant survived. That single plant was incredibly fruitful, one might say self-fertile, and within 50 years had more than 18 million progeny.

Sex and seedlings, Coffee comes to Brazil

While the love story of Coffee and de Clieu was tender and beautiful, this was not the only incident where Coffee was involved in an affair of the heart. Actually this was a little different, but still driven by a burning desire for coffee. Imagine a corporate spy, or perhaps James Bond with a Portugese accent. We are now in Brazil and this is 1727. Brazil's government wants a cut of the coffee market. They hire this corporate James Bond to obtain some seeds. Enter Lt. Col. Francisco de Melo Palheta, a Brazilian coffee fanatic. This very attractive young man is sent to French Guiana on a diplomatic assignment. Some of the offspring from the Coffee de Clieu brought to Martinique were now bringing enlightenment and commerce to the small colony of French Guiana, bordering Brazil.

Lt. Col. Francisco de Melo Palheta is sent with the stated mission of negotiating a minor border dispute, but his real objective was to obtain and smuggle out of this French colony enough live coffee beans to introduce us to the beautiful Brazilian hillsides. Unfortunately, the plantations in French Guiana were like fortresses, heavily guarded with armed troops.

This dashing young officer-diplomat-spy decided on a ploy that's the stuff movies and novels are made of. Hummmmm. I may have to write another book. Back to this true story of intrigue, passion and deception. The governor of French Guiana was an older man with a beautiful, young wife who was also a witty young lady, and as bright as she was charming. She was swept off her feet by this handsome intellectual in uniform. Francisco saw an opportunity and requested that she give him a tour of the coffee plantations, since her husband was occupied with affairs of state.

After a series of clandestine amorous meetings, she agreed to secure some coffee seeds for him. Unfortunately this was a greater challenge than she had anticipated. She had to admit failure and bade him a sorrowful farewell and regretfully stated she would not see him again.

He had succeeded in negotiating a treaty that put an end to the minor boundary dispute, and the Governor hosted a state farewell dinner to celebrate the agreement. While he was dressing for this event, a note from the governor's wife was delivered. After the dinner, as he was preparing to leave, she met him at the door. He kissed her hand as a good diplomat would do, and she presented him with a token of appreciation for negotiating the dispute to a favorable conclusion. This token was a huge bouquet of roses. As she handed these flowers to him, she gave him a kiss on the cheek and whispered, "Thank you for the gift of your presence in our palace. Don't unwrap these roses until you have crossed the border." Then she turned and was gone.

He was puzzled by this and expected a love letter, or perhaps a thank you note. The carriage ride over the rough road prevented any napping, or pleasant dreams. After several hours they approached the border, and the armed guard left to return to the capital. Lt. Col. Francisco de Melo Palheta was greeted by the Brazilian escort with a bottle of wine. As they shared the drink and a few jokes, one of the soldiers asked about the enormous bouquet of roses. Francisco carefully unwrapped them to retrieve the anticipated note. As he began to separate the flowers, several dozen coffee seedlings were revealed. From these, the result of an illicit romantic encounter, sprouted the world's greatest coffee empire, and a great song by Frank Sinatra.

Unfortunately, the coffee industry was dependent on slaves, and in the first half of the 19th century 1.5 million slaves were imported to Brazil to provide labor for the coffee plantations. By 1800, Brazil's monster harvests would turn coffee from an elite indulgence to an everyday elixir, a drink for the people, the pathway to universal enlightenment.

1732 Classical humor

Throughout Europe, drinking songs were popular. Often these were vulgar, obscene or offensive to any coffee lover's sense of decency. Fortunately, as my Coffee relatives replaced the consumption of fermented beverages, more inspirational and civilized music became common. In Germany, even Johann Sebastian Bach got caught up in the coffee culture movement. He composed the earlier mentioned humorous *Coffee Cantata*. It's the story of a befuddled father who tries to get his headstrong and rebellious teenage daughter to kick the coffee habit and get married.

It's a tough choice, coffee or marriage? The composition is said to have been inspired by a conversation Bach had with one of his own daughters. It was first performed in Zimmerman's Coffee House in Germany, where he often practiced and performed.

Lyrics to Bach's Kaffee Kantate (Coffee Cantata)

Recitative Narrator
Be quiet, stop chattering, and pay attention to what's taking place: here comes Herr Schlendrian with his daughter Lieschen; he's growling like a honey bear. Hear for yourselves, what she has done to him!

Aria - Schlendrian
Don't one's children cause one endless trials & tribulations!
What I say each day to my daughter Lieschen falls on stony ground.

Recitative - Schlendrian
You wicked child, you disobedient girl,
Oh! when will I get my way; give up coffee!

Lieschen
Father, don't be so severe! If I can't drink my bowl of coffee three times daily, then in my torment I will shrivel up like a piece of roast goat.

Aria - Lieschen
Mm! how sweet the coffee tastes, more delicious than a thousand kisses, mellower than muscatel wine. Coffee, coffee I must have,
and if someone wishes to give me a treat, ah, then pour me out some coffee!

Recitative - Schlendrian
If you don't give up drinking coffee then you shan't go to any wedding feast, nor go out walking. Oh! When will I get my way; give up coffee!

Lieschen
Oh well! Just leave me my coffee!

Schlendrian
Now I've got the little minx!
I won't get you a whalebone skirt in the latest fashion.

Lieschen
I can easily live with that.

Schlendrian
You're not to stand at the window and watch people pass by!

Lieschen
That as well, only I beg of you, leave me my coffee!

Schlendrian
Furthermore,
you shan't be getting any silver or gold ribbon for your bonnet from me!

Lieschen
Yes, yes! only leave me to my pleasure!

Schlendrian
You disobedient Lieschen you, so you go along with it all!

Aria - Schlendrian
Hard-hearted girls are not so easily won over.
Yet if one finds their weak spot, ah! Then one comes away successful.

Recitative - Schlendrian
Now take heed what your father says!

Lieschen
In everything but the coffee.

Schlendrian
Well then, you'll have to resign yourself to never taking a husband.

Lieschen
Oh yes! Father, a husband!

Schlendrian
I swear it won't happen.

Lieschen
Until I can forgo coffee? From now on, coffee, remain forever untouched!
Father, listen, I won't drink any.

Schlendrian
Then you shall have a husband at last!

Aria - Lieschen
Today even dear father, see to it! Oh, a husband! Really, that suits me splendidly!
If it could only happen soon that at last, before I go to bed,
instead of coffee I were to get a proper lover!

Recitative - Narrator
Old Schlendrian goes off to see if he can find a husband forthwith for his daughter
Lieschen; but Lieschen secretly lets it be known: no suitor is to come to my house
unless he promises me, and it is also written into the marriage contract, that I will
be permitted to make myself coffee whenever I want.

Trio
A cat won't stop from catching mice, and maidens remain faithful to their coffee.
The mother holds her coffee dear, the grandmother drank it also,
who can thus rebuke the daughters!

There are numerous recordings and videos of the Coffee Cantata available.

Chapter 3
Coffee, The Beverage of Revolution

Some dared refer to us as "that revolting beverage"

At first we assumed that North America was too cold and rural for colonization by coffee, but it soon became evident that while these humans, both those who already resided in the pristine beauty of this continent, and those who "discovered" it, were enthusiastic about consuming well-brewed coffee and reveled in the liberation of the mind that we provided. It was obvious that we had some great opportunities on this continent.

First I must dispel one of the great myths that persists even to this enlightened day. The people of the seaboard colonies may have drunk great quantities of "tea" when coffee was unavailable. However, much of this tea was brewed from native plants and was used for medicinal purposes. There was sassafras tea, birch tea, strawberry tea, and the list could continue for pages. The tea from distant ports was a commercial enterprise, subsidized by the British government, much like oil is today. This is part of the reason for the famous tea party held in Boston in 1773. More about this soon.

The original inhabitants, the First People of North America, had their own version of coffee, so it was only natural that they would take great delight in sipping the brew from the fruit of our Coffee trees. The "black drink," as they called their elixir steeped from the leaves of several species of holly, was bitter but sufficiently caffeine-enriched to free the mind from the mundane, and prepare these folks for discussion on topics of importance.

The Yupon and Dahoon holly were both indigenous sources of caffeine in North America, but when they encountered real coffee in the coffee houses in the colonial settlements, they frequently became patrons. Perhaps it was because Native Americans gathered in the colonial coffee houses that the Mohawk people inspired the grandest tea party of all time. I must add that in South America the first choice was yerba mate, a similar caffeine-rich drink from another holly called *Ilex paraguariensis*. This was served in small ceremonial gourds, now often decorated with beautiful silver, and drank through special metal straws that allow the pure liquid through, straining out all the leaves.

Back to Boston. After a series of corporate lobbying efforts on the part of the East India Tea Company. The British Parliament gave this tea company a combination of special subsidies and the customers a special tea tax. This gave this corporation an unprecedented advantage over the other beverages available to the colonies.

Keep in mind, coffee was enjoyed by Europeans, including the British and the colonists, before tea became available as an inferior substitute for our unequaled beverage. Tea is nothing more than weakly flavored water that fails completely in enlightening and domesticating you humans we took pity on so many centuries ago. Without the power of coffee, humanity would never have advanced to the point where they could comprehend the potential we envisoned for their minds, or our ability to improve your behavior. Nor could they have gained the intellectual capacity to invent coffee roasters, the French Press, complex espresso machines and the enterprising artistry of coffee mugs. Not to mention the coffee industry that developed without any form of corporate welfare from most governments.

While we call it the Boston Tea Party, it was inspired by the COFFEE consumed by the organizers of the Occupy Boston group in 1773 as a response to a series of acts designed to promote the profits of the tea industry. I completely agree that tea, being an inferior beverage, needed special support to compete, or even survive. But, when a group of true intellectuals devoted to Coffee joined together, history was made. They met in the Green Dragon Coffee House, still open today, and with the assistance of many pots of fresh, steaming hot coffee, the plan was devised.

Daniel Webster described this historic coffeehouse as "the headquarters of the Revolution." Samuel Adams, John Adams, James Otis, Paul Revere and many other intellectual leaders of the time met there to explore avenues to secure their rights with the aid and wisdom gained from good coffee. The Green Dragon was a modest two story brick building with a steep roof and leaded windows. Over the door was a sign picturing a large green dragon and a sign in the window proclaimed "The Best Coffee in Boston."

These Occupy Boston protestors at first wanted to march as an armed band onto the ships carrying tea, now anchored in the harbor. The plan was to mass on the dock and deliver a series of speeches to the local media. Then, they would set fire to the tea-laden vessels and go back to the Green Dragon.

The story told by my ancestors and respected Coffee historians is different from the one found in the American history books. One of the Native American patrons of the Green Dragon suggested that they use more peaceful methods. He was able to help the Occupy Boston membership dress in contemporary Mohawk fashion and arm themselves only with small hatchets symbolizing tomahawks. Rather than committing acts of violence, they approached the captains of the three vessels in the harbor, the Dartmouth, Eleanor and Beaver, armed with reason and logic.

The estimated 130 coffee drinkers then began what amounted to a lengthy lecture on free enterprise, the value of fair and open competition, and even passed out free cups of coffee. This rather one sided conversation continued for hours. Finally, the exhausted captains handed the protestors the keys to the cargo holds and retired to their quarters.

In less than three hours, this band of informal activists/educators had taken the 342 chests of East India Tea, smashed the lids with their hatchets and dumped the crates and contents overboard. This peaceful and rational teach-in, which later came to be known as the Boston Tea Party, made drinking coffee the right and logical thing to do throughout the colonies.

Coffee later became the patriotic beverage of a new nation. It could be said, in fact I will say it. "The American War of Independence" was inspired, fueled and celebrated with coffee. In fact, Coffee has quite a revolutionary history. Read on.

Abigail Adams and the Boston Coffee Party

On July 31, 1777, Abigail Adams wrote to her husband John, who was busy creating a new nation at the Continental Congress in Philadelphia.

"I have nothing new to entertain you with, unless it is an account of a New Set of Nobility which have lately taken the Lead in Boston. You must know that there is a great Scarcity of Sugar and Coffee, articles which the Female part of the State are very loth to give up, especially whilst they consider the Scarcity occasioned by the merchants having secreted a large quantity. There has been much rout and noise in the town for several weeks. Some stores had been opened by a number of people and the Coffee and Sugar carried into the Market and dealt out by pounds.

"It was rumoured that an eminent, wealthy, stingy Merchant (who is a bachelor) had a Hogshead of Coffee in his store which he refused to sell to the committee under 6 shillings per pound. A Number of Females some say a hundred, some say more, assembled with a cart and trucks, marched down to the warehouse and demanded the keys, which he refused to deliver, upon which one of them seized him by his neck and tossed him into the cart. Upon his finding no quarter he delivered the keys, when they tipped up the cart and discharged him, then opened the warehouse, hoisted out the Coffee themselves, put it into the trucks and drove off. It was reported that he had a spanking among them, but this I believe was not true. A large concourse of Men stood amazed, silent spectators of the whole transaction."

I demand equal time in the history books. Boston Tea Party indeed.

George Washington & Thomas Jefferson
and how they were inspired by my Coffee relatives

It wasn't only Boston where coffee was able to influence events. Richard Charlton, a local wig maker and coffee afficionado, opened a coffeehouse in Williamsburg, Virginia. Today, in a tourist attraction known as Colonial Williamsburg, Charlton's Coffee House has reopened on the original historic site. George Washington and Thomas Jefferson frequently stopped by for coffee and conversation at Charlton's. They and other intellectuals gathered to discuss ideas, philosophy and politics over delicious and stimulating coffee.

In Philadelphia, the London Coffee House was the gathering place of the Occupy Pennsylvania protestors. Similar groups gathered at coffee houses from New York to Savanna. The Declaration of Independence was read in front of the Merchant's Coffee House in Philadelphia, one of Ben Franklin's favorite meeting places. Early in the war the Continental Congress declared coffee the national drink.

Coffeehouses throughout the colonies became the gathering places for not only intellectuals, writers, artists and statesmen, but businessmen and investors as well. History was made in New York in the Merchants Coffee House on Wall Street. One beautiful spring day, inspired by a rich morning coffee, a group of men met in the shade of a huge sycamore, commonly referred to as a Buttonwood, on Wall Street and wrote a set of rules they would use to trade and invest. This became known as the Buttonwood Agreement. It was in the 1790's that coffee was finally able to organize the fledgling American business community into a legitimate exchange.

Haiti and the American Revolution

My ancestors worked hard to promote liberty, freedom, democracy and humanity. In fact Coffee has been called "the catalyst of Revolution" by numerous human historians. The revolting activity of thirteen colonies was only the beginning. Let's look at some additional ways Coffee played a role in your domestication and enlightenment.

Do you know what nation was the world leader in coffee production in 1776? Of course you don't, so I'll tell you. It was the french colony of Haiti. Do you remember our discussion of Gabriel de Clieu who brought coffee seedlings to Martinique in the 1720's? By the 1750's the Jesuits introduced some of the offspring from de Clieu's cherished plants to Haiti. By the 1770's Haitian coffee was influencing thought and promoting revolutionary ideas in

Boston, New York, Philadelphia, Williamsburg and other cities in these thirteen colonies

Because of the world's taste for coffee, French colonial plantations relied heavily on African slave laborers. By1788, Haiti supplied half the world's coffee. The brutal treatment of the slaves led to a series of violent revolts, and in 1804 the first successful slave revolt in the western hemisphere made Haiti an independent nation.

I am very proud of the people who were creating this new nation, the United States of America, although they did make some mistakes, and these humans continue to err even today. We have to keep in mind that they aren't fully domesticated yet. Americans, and all humans, are best considered a work in progress.

When they were looking for a name for this new country, we had hoped that we might get some credit for our efforts. I have been told that some at the Continental Congress had advocated calling this the Coffee Republic. It has been claimed that one of my ancestors, Benjamin Coffea, had proposed The United States of Coffee, but, alas, the majority insisted on USA. There was nothing we could do. As trees, we were, and still are, denied the right to vote.

By 1790 coffee imports to the new United States of America were 30% greater than tea, and less that a decade later, coffee consumption was ten times that of tea. I am content in the knowledge that America is only a part of Coffee's manifest destiny, and it is our mission to continue this, our civilizing and enlightening efforts. This has been a rocky road with numerous setbacks, but there is no use crying over spilled coffee. We must carry on.

Aloha, Coffee comes to Hawaii

The ride through the district of Kona to Kealakekua Bay took us through the famous coffee section. I think Kona coffee has a richer flavor than any other be it grown where it may. Mark Twain.

Certainly, he was one of America's most creative writers, although some might not consider him fully domesticated. He was definitely enlightened and inspired by the coffee he consumed. This comment can be found in his *Letters from Hawaii* written in 1866.

I speak for the Coffee seeds and seedlings who were the first to arrive on the island of Oah'u. We thoroughly enjoyed our introduction to Hawaii. The climate, the soil and the people were all delightful. This earliest attempt was by the capable and witty Don Francisco de Paula y Marin, the Spanish doctor/interpreter and advisor to King Kamehameha II. In 1813 his attempt to bring us to this island paradise was a failure. But we didn't let this little setback stop us in our efforts to domesticate all humans. Perhaps I should note that Don Francisco introduced two plants in that year. The coffee failed but the second species was very successful, and became a primary crop throughout the Hawaiian islands. This was, of course, the pineapple. It may be healthy, but it certainly can't be considered a part of the human enlightenment project.

In 1825 King Kamehameha II and his Queen decided to visit England. Unfortunately, during this vacation they both contracted measles. This disease proved fatal for both the Hawaiian monarch and his spouse. Governor/Chief Boki arranged for their bodies to be returned to the Island on the H.M.S. Blonde. While the ship stopped in Rio de Janeiro for cargo and provisions, Chief Boki was able to purchase a small number of young coffee plants. Do you remember Lt. Col. Francisco de Melo Palheta, the Brazilian diplomat and his brief affair with the wife of the Governor of French Guiana? These coffee plants were the, should we say, "illegitimate" offspring from that fling.

On reaching Hawaii, these seedlings were planted and nurtured by John Wilkinson. It was unfortunate that, because we are such beautiful alluring plants with charming flowers that produce such an enticing fragrance, Mr. Wilkinson grew them as ornamentals. Reverend Samuel Ruggles moved some of these trees to Kona in 1828. The Hanalei Valley on the North Shore of Kauai was home to the first coffee plantation in Hawaii.

Kona is a special member of my family, a Brazilian *Coffea arabica*. I have to admit that I am proud of Kona. She grows a little farther north than most coffee, and this may influence the fine flavor of the Kona beans. She blooms in February and March. These multitudes of small white flowers, we call them Kona Snow, cover the tree and perfume the air. Young fruit called berries form in about a month or two. By late August, these green berries begin to turn a delightful red and we call them cherries at this mature stage. This means it's time to harvest. This is done by hand, carefully and gently with the respect due a fruit whose destiny is the continued domestication, enlightenment and empowerment of all humanity. This process is repeated several times because all of these cherries do not ripen at once and we certainly don't want them picked before their time. That can affect the flavor and limit our ability to influence the course of human events.

Bet you didn't know this. Each Kona Coffee tree produces about fifteen pounds of cherries, but this means about two pounds of coffee beans when cleaned and roasted. Now, how many cups of gourmet coffee is that? Better question, "How many great ideas can be found in a pound of Kona coffee?"

44

Chapter 4
From Gold Rush to Civil War
"The Best Part of Wakin' Up is Folgers in Your Cup®"

In 1849, gold was accidently discovered in the hills behind San Francisco, and the rush was on. The general Coffee wisdom was that this was not the time or place to promote civility or intellectual pursuits. But, in 1850, a young man named William Bovee had different ideas. He decided that the best way to mine gold was with a coffee cup. At the same time, a family from Massachusetts had sent their three sons to California. The youngest of these was a fifteen-year-old boy named James. While his brothers headed for the hills, James had to work for the money needed to provision his brothers and himself in their quest for gold.

Coffee had inspired Mr. Bovee to start a business called The Pioneer Steam Coffee and Spice Mills. He was in need of a carpenter, and James was in need of a job. Mr. Bovee had been inspired by the coffee he consumed, so inspired that he had a great idea. Yes. I confess, we had a hand, or should I say a leaf, in this process. You see, coffee beans were bought raw, the proper term is green, and roasted when humans were ready to make a pot of coffee. Bovee developed a way to roast and grind the green beans and package them in convenient metal cans.

After helping build the Pioneer Steam Coffee Mill, James had enough money to join his brothers in the gold fields. Finally, being cold, hungry and poor for several years, James was sitting by the fire filled with despair while the last of his coffee was brewing. It was with this final cup of inspiration that he made a decision. Yes! Of course we helped him, but he does deserve some of the credit. After all, his name was James Folger. He returned to San Francisco. The rest is history.

Cowboy Coffee

Generations ago, back before cowboys sipped their coffee in the neighborhood coffeehouse, there was this curious concoction known as Scandinavian egg coffee. My editor and good friend Tomi made some as a special treat for Hank. I must admit when they tried this *egg coffee* they told me that it was "interesting." Tomi says it's quite easy to make and she was kind enough to share the recipe for my book. I don't think Juan Valdez ever made coffee this way. I like to think of it as Campfire Coffee, the great companion to warm s'mores. There are many variations on this theme, including one Cowboy Coffee recipe that calls for the boiling of the coffee grounds for some time before adding the egg as the last step before actually drinking it. I must make this perfectly clear. Neither cowboys nor Norskes are likely to brew their coffee this way today, but it's fun to try it, at least once.

Tomi tells me this is a tradition in Lutheran church gatherings of Scandinavian-Americans in the Midwest. They are rumored to serve it with lutefisk. Perhaps I need to explain to those of you who aren't from a Scandinavian cultural tradition. This is a white fish soaked in lye until it assumes the consistency of Jell-O and what can only be described as an AWESOME aroma. This is a part of the traditional Thanksgiving dinner in such remote parts of the world as Minnesota. Some view it as a religious ritual and I have been told that "it can be either an act of faith to eat that stuff, or an act of wisdom to pass on it and go straight to the coffee." Either way, these Norskes and their cousins, the Laughing Swedes, are famous for their coffee, and this is the true religious experience.

What you need to make Campfire Coffee:
9 coffee cups of water to boil
1 1/4 coffee cups of cold water
3/4 coffee cup freshly ground coffee, medium or coarse grind work
1 egg

Boiling your Scandinavian Egg Coffee:
1. Bring the 9 cups of water to a rapid boil in a saucepan or enamel coffee pot.
2. Meanwhile, stir together ground coffee, 1/4 cup water, and 1 egg
Note: diehard egg coffee lovers use the crushed eggshell as well, but it works fine to leave this out. When ready, I think the mixture looks like potting soil.
3. Heat the water to boiling.
4. Now carefully pour in the egg-coffee mixture. You may need to move the pot back from the flames or turn down the heat to prevent it from boiling over. Boil the coffee for 3 minutes. Note: You'll see that the coffee grounds will gradually bind together into a single mass that floats at the top of the pot. When Tomi did this I began to worry. Then I was surprised.
5. Remove pot from the fire and pour in 1 cup cold water. Let the coffee settle for 10 minutes. Now for the surprise. The "lump" of grounds slowly settles to the bottom of the pot.
6. Pour through a strainer into tin camp cups and serve. The flavor of the coffee grows stronger, without becoming bitter, the longer that it simmers.

Coffee and the Civil War

Throughout the Civil War, coffee was a prized commodity on the battlefields and in the halls of government. I have heard stories, as a young plant sitting at my mother's roots, that when the Union troops were marching, they would often chew on roasted coffee beans to provide the energy to keep moving. When camp was made for the night, the first order of business was to start the campfires and get the coffee on. From a distance these encampments gave the appearance of a thousand dots of light, or a very large flock of fireflies.

Coffee was a rare commodity for both the Union and the Confederate armies. This meant they were often forced to use those dreaded substitutes.

In the South one of the most common was called Peanut Coffee, but you know as well as I do, THERE IS NO SUBSTITUTE FOR REAL COFFEE. This peanut concoction even had a recipe that was circulated among the Confederate troops. For a pot of this foul stuff, you had to mix a half cup each of peanuts, cow peas and raw wheat. Then it was roasted until a rich brown color prevailed. At this point you could grind this unwholesome mixture and brew it over an open fire. Then as a test of courage you could drink it. If you dared. I assure you that Coffee had nothing to do with this, but could it be that this Peanut Coffee could have influenced the outcome of this conflict?

Chicory was also popular, but dandelion roots and toasted grains from rye to rice were frequently used. In one journal, roasted bread crusts or biscuits were said to make a poor, but acceptable, substitute, but not as bad as watermelon seeds. Acorns, skillet parched, were perhaps second to chicory root and were said to be passable on a cold night. More on this subject of substitutes later.

Letters home from the battlefield

Those wearing the uniforms of both sides frequently displayed the influence coffee had on their minds. They were incurable romantics, consummate story tellers and compulsive writers. Soldiers kept journals, wrote letters home almost non-stop, and enjoyed conversation. The following letter is a good example of the advanced domestication we had achieved by the 1860's.

Yankee soldier John F. Brobst of the Twenty-fifth Wisconsin Volunteer Infantry wrote his sweetheart in an 1864 letter posted from somewhere near Atlanta.

We had two visitors day before yesterday. They were Johnny Rebs They came over and took dinner with us and brought over some corn bread and tobacco and we made some coffee and all sat down on the ground together and had a good chat as well as a good dinner. They gave us some tobacco and we gave them some coffee to take back with them. They were real smart fellows both of them. You must not think up there that we fight down here because we are mad, for it is not the case, for we pick blackberries together and off the same bush at the same time, but we fight for fun, or rather because we can't help ourselves. If they would let the soldiers settle this thing it would not be long before we would be on terms of peace.

A monument to coffee and the Battle of Antietam

As the troops for both sides prepared for the bloodiest single day of battle in this war, it was a cold, dark day with rain and fog. The forests and fields around the community of Sharpsburg, MD were literally crawling with soldiers, all in desperate need of coffee. This was the Battle of Antietam and the date was Sept 17, 1862. But, let's step back a day for a glimpse at how difficult life was for the young boys preparing for battle in the morning.

Pvt. David L. Thompson, a soldier from the 9th NY Infantry, made camp the day before this critical battle that Lincoln needed to win before he could issue the Emancipation Proclamation a few months later. Late in the day before this infamous battle, Pvt. Thompson took his place on the Union line and opened his bed roll. He sat is the cold and wrote in a letter home, *"We sat down and watched for a while the dull glare on the sky of the Confederate campfires behind the hills," Thompson wrote. "We were hungry, of course, but as no fires were allowed, we could only mix our ground coffee and sugar in our hands and eat them dry . . . There was something weirdly impressive yet unreal in the gradual drawing together of those whispering armies under cover of the night—something of awe and dread."*

Coffee obviously played a major role in this conflict. While no one has thought to write a book, or even make a movie honoring our efforts to make the soldier's life easier and bring slavery to an end, there is a monument. It's a beautiful battlefield monument honoring the inspiration of coffee, and the courage of an obscure Ohio Commissary Sergeant in the Ohio Volunteer Infantry, for supplying coffee to the troops during battle. Soldiers who remembered the deed paid for the memorial recognizing this unusual and courageous act.

Coffee Bill was what they called this 19-year-old school teacher from Niles, Ohio. This young Commissary Sergeant was relatively safe stationed well behind the shifting battle lines with the necessary provisions and supplies. The men of the Twenty-third rushed into battle before dawn, and this meant they were engaged before their morning coffee, and the battle raged through the day. With exceptional initiative, this sergeant gathered a work detail of volunteers, commandeered a couple of mule-drawn wagons, one of which was a mobile field kitchen, and moved all quickly into harm's way transporting cooked rations and buckets filled with precious fresh boiled coffee.

It is said that young Sergeant William McKinley, a.k.a. Coffee Bill, bravely risked his life as he passed through artillery fire and delivered, with his own hands, the coffee so essential for the men for whom he was laboring. I think it was this infusion of coffee that empowered the union forces to claim victory that day. Later this school teacher and coffee hero became the 25th president of the United States.

He was assassinated in 1901 by Leon Czolgosz, an anarchist who most likely wasn't a fan of fine coffee and its civilizing influences. In 1903 a monument to Coffee, William McKinley and his front-line coffee service was dedicated on the Antietam Battlefield adjacent to the parking lot south of Burnside Bridge. An inscription on the memorial notes that Sgt. McKinley "personally and without orders served hot coffee and warm food to every man in the Regiment, on this spot, and in doing so had to pass under fire." One section of the monument shows McKinley, hot cup of coffee in hand, with shells bursting all around him.

Coffee was the healthiest thing the soldiers could drink

One of my heroes from this time period was Florence Nightingale. She was British and developed nursing programs for the battlefield hospitals of the Crimean War. She also served as a consultant to the Union in the American Civil War. She encouraged the U.S. Sanitary Commission to serve coffee rather than water in the hospitals, infirmaries, and commissaries. This was because the boiling process used to make coffee killed germs that caused dysentery and other diseases. I hesitate to point this out, but there were almost twice as many deaths from disease as marksmanship. This was true on both sides. These soldiers were COFFEE DRINKERS and far better at creative and intellectual endeavors such as writing love letters and entries in their journals, sketching the scenery and composing verse, than anything as crude as fighting.

Clara Barton is known as the founder of the American Red Cross, but we call her the Coffee Angel of the battlefield, camp and hospital. She mustered the courage to go to these places where the wounded were suffering and served them coffee, crackers and soup. When she wasn't serving the desperately needed coffee, she was distributing bandages, clean clothing and kind words. She was much inspired by Florence and trained those nursing the wounded troops on the importance of sanitation, and coffee.

These nursing practices, along with the appreciation of coffee, moved from the camp and battlefield to the homesteads, family farms and small towns of this growing nation. A poet with questionably spelling ability wrote this in 1874.

Like His Mother Used to Make
James Whitcomb Riley, *Uncle Jake's Place*

"I was born in Indiany," says a stranger, lank and slim,
As us fellers in the restarunt was kindo' guyin' him,
And Uncle Jake was slidin' him another punkin pie
And a' extry cup o' coffee, with a twinkle in his eye.
"I was born in Indiany-- more'n forty year' ago--
I hain't be'n back in twenty-- and I'm workin' back'ards slow;
But I've et in ever' restarunt 'twixt here and Santy Fee,
And I want to state this coffee tastes like gittin' home, to me!"

"Pour us out another, Daddy," says the feller, warmin' up,
A-speakin' 'cost a saucerful, as Uncle tuk his cup--,
"When I seed yer sign out yander," he went on, to Uncle Jake- -,
"'Come in and git some coffee like yer mother used to make'--
I thought of my old mother, and the Posey County farm,
And me a little kid ag'in, a-hangin' in her arm,
As she set the pot: a-bilin', broke the eggs and poured 'em in--"
And the feller kindo' halted, with a trimble in his chin:

And Uncle Jake he fetched the feller's coffee back, and stood
As solemn, fer a minute, as a' undertaker would;
Then he sorto' turned and tiptoed to'rds the kitchen door-- and nex',
Here comes his old wife out with him, a-rubbin' of her specs--
And she rushes fer the stranger, and she hollers out, "It's him--!
Thank God we've met him comin'--! Don't you know, yer mother, Jim?"
And the feller, as he grabbed her, says--, "You bet I hain't forgot--
But," wipin' of his eyes, says he, "yer coffee's mighty hot!"

Chapter 5:
From Arbuckle's to Sinatra

I believe humans get a lot done, not because we're smart, but because we have thumbs so we can make coffee. Flash Rosenberg

The history of humanity, since the middle of the 19th century until tomorrow, is a history of grand invention and creative enterprise. The following is a brief discussion of what can happen when the genius of Coffee empowers the industry of humanity. These are only a few of the tools we developed to support our symbiotic relationship with humankind. I must explain that we try to be subtle so that the humans think these ideas are their own. As you can see from my skills as a writer, I am very modest and avoid any attempt to take any credit personally for all these grand ideas that have made your progress possible.

I am Coffee, not the purveyor of progress, only the inspiration and the catalyst for a better future, not the one doing the labor. That, after all, is for those with opposable thumbs. We in the plant kingdom have leaves, and those of us who can call ourselves Coffee use our leaves to turn solar energy into coffee energy. This is why you are so willing to use your back and those curious appendages you call thumbs to make us happy. Just saying . . .

It's fascinating to see the unfolding of our inspiring thoughts within the minds of the humans we have empowered. What a dynamic thing the human mind can become, when driven by Coffee. One good idea, planted and nurtured, grows and produces many beautiful and diverse fruits. We Coffees have a saying, "The human mind is a garden of flowers waiting for Coffee to give it the courage to blossom." In the past 100 years, each idea we planted produced many fruits, as one inspired idea led to another, and on, and on.

The first of these great creative events occurred as the Civil War was becoming a history lesson. Throughout this horrendous conflict, boiling the coffee was both a challenge and an art form. It started with green coffee beans. These are coffee seeds that haven't been roasted. Immediately before making the hot, life-sustaining beverage, these beans had to be roasted on a stove or in a skillet over a campfire prior to being ground and used. That was until we inspired the owners of a neighborhood grocery store.

Two brothers, John and Charles Arbuckle, were partners in a family grocery business in Pittsburgh, PA. They changed the course of history by developing and patenting a process to seal in our unique flavor and aroma. Let's take a look at how these events transpired.

"Have an Arbuckle"

John and Charles Arbuckle were true coffee enthusiasts. We helped them create a process for roasting, then coating coffee beans with a glaze made from sugar and egg whites to lock in the flavor until needed. I must admit that, as the primary ingredient in this process, we did enjoy that sugar coating. Then, we helped these brothers invent a machine that filled, sealed and labeled coffee in paper bags. They called it *Arbuckle Ariosa*. This became the first mass produced and mass marketed coffee. Eventually the Arbuckles became the largest importer of coffee in the US. They soon became one of the largest ship owners in America because they owned a fleet of merchant vessels engaged in the South American coffee trade.

Arbuckles' was called *The coffee that won the west*. This was no idle boast on our part. It is the truth. Some may think it was the six gun, but the reality is that it was Coffee that tamed the Wild, Wild West.

We even helped them with a radical new idea, a most clever way to use the power of Coffee to open and engage the human mind. In each package of coffee were collector cards with pictures of animals, birds, plants and people. It is a part of our Coffee legend, told in the stories we share around the campfires and warm winter fireplaces even today. Sometimes we will laugh so hard we shake our leaves when an elder tree will tell us of the cowboys who would drink coffee and trade these cards. So eager were they to amass complete sets that they would prefer them to money as the winnings in that ingenious mental sport they devised called Poker. After all, money was spent and gone, but what they learned from these cards stayed with them forever.

These are considered valuable antique collector items today, as the value of knowledge always increases with time. You may have noticed that this concept was adapted by the makers of bubble gum as a way to encourage children to engage in heathy exercise. Our work with the Arbuckles' coffee company inspired the creation of baseball cards. We Coffees are proud of the way humans are able to share and adapt the good ideas we give them. Sometimes you can be quite clever. We have always had a good deal of confidence in you humans.

"Who wants the candy?" was another brilliant idea we gave the Arbuckle brothers. This one was later adapted by the makers of Cracker Jacks and breakfast cereals with great success. But Arbuckles' was the first to put a little surprise in every package. Cowboys out on the trail, or simply doing whatever it was they did before smart phones, had little access to candy. So, including a peppermint stick inside each bag of coffee was a true stroke of genius. When the chuck wagon cook was ready to make coffee, he would call out to the awakening trail hands "Who wants the candy?" It was the cowboy who ground the coffee who earned the candy.

Sensing that we were on a roll, we gave the Arbuckle brothers one more ingenious idea. Actually, it was two ideas. Do you remember S & H Green Stamps? While John and Charles were sharing a midmorning cup of coffee, we slipped a dime novel onto the table. In it was a story about a cowboy who was trying to save enough money for a wedding ring for the gal he was sweet on.

"What if we printed a coupon on the Ariosa bags?" John spoke while refilling his coffee cup.

"Why?" Charles replied, enjoying the conversation that always accompanied this other invention of theirs we now call a "Coffee Break."

"I was reading about this poor boy who was struggling to save money for a wedding ring. Unfortunately he had to keep dipping into his savings for bandanas, razors, a pocket knife and a new tin coffee cup."

Charles looked at his brother. "You want to send him a gold wedding ring? What's that got to do with our coffee bags?"

"There are folks all over the country drinking our coffee. You and I both know that Folgers and other folks are going to want a share of the business. We need a way to make our customers loyal to us. If we give them these coupons, they can save them up until they get so many and then send them to us and we send them a razor, or pocket knife or good book to read, or a collection of our cards, or, yes, even a wedding ring."

By now John had finished his third cup of Ariosa and was already sketching the design for this new idea. From there it was just a short hop of imagination to the Green Stamps, Gold Bond Stamps and a number of other saving stamps. Imitation is the sincerest form of flattery, and later the US government modified the idea and called it Savings Bonds. We Coffees are so clever.

"Good to the Last Drop"

In Nashville, Tennessee there was a hotel. In 1884 a traveling salesman named Joel Cheek finally settled in Nashville, a place he had visited often in his travels. He had become a self-educated expert on Coffee. Until this time Coffee was marketed by its point of origin, rather than brand names or special blends. But at least a decade earlier, Joel began experimenting, mixing a little of this and a little of that, all the while keeping notes on the results. His goal was to create just the perfect blend of flavor and aroma.

When he moved to this delightful city, he frequented this hotel, and sitting in the dining room one afternoon he chanced to meet a British coffee expert, Roger Nolley Smith. They dined often at the hotel and became the best of friends. They worked together on Joel's quest for the perfect blend, and Eureka! They found it, with a little help from us. Soon their blend became the house coffee for the hotel and they formed the Nashville Coffee Company. While we tried to discourage them, vanity got in the way and they soon renamed their company the Cheek Neal Coffee Company. The house blend for the hotel became their most famous brand. Seven presidents had stayed at this famous hotel and in 1907 one of them, Theodore Roosevelt, was said to have made a comment supposedly overheard by a reporter in the dining room one evening. It soon became the advertising slogan for the best blend of the Cheek Neal Coffee Co. "Good to the last drop" was what he said. The place was The Maxwell Hotel. Maxwell House Coffee was the first blended coffee to be marketed in the United States. There are many versions of this story, some stating that TR's cup of Maxwell Coffee was consumed at Andrew Jackson's estate, the Hermitage. Others claim it was the work of a creative advertising manager.

A New Era for Coffee

1900 was the dawning of a new century for coffee, coffee drinkers and a couple more inspired and enterprising brothers. Reuben and Austin came to San Francisco in 1878 and bought The Arabian Coffee, Tea and Spice Company, a food distributor selling dairy goods, coffee, tea, spices and other grocery items. Because Coffee is such a social plant, we encourage both coffee drinkers and dealers to enjoy proximity as well. The Arabian Coffee Co. was just a couple blocks from Folgers. It's easier for us to keep track of them this way.

We spent many mornings in the office with RW (Reuben) and Austin, encouraging them and liberating their minds as we prepared them for the next great idea. Perhaps I need to explain a little about how we viewed our responsibilities to you and your fellow coffee patrons of the world. We led you to the coffee cup, encouraged your minds and developed your taste for our delightful beverage. Our first goal, Coffee growing around the world, was already a reality. Our second goal of Coffee in every house, was becoming a serious possibility. But, we were cautious not to put all our beans in one coffee pot. Humans sometimes say "all your eggs in one basket," but they copied our cautionary wisdom.

The problem was keeping the roasted coffee fresh until brewed. We were working with several creative humans whose minds we had liberated. The Norton brothers in Chicago were working on a vacuum process. James Sanborn and Caleb Chase in Boston were the first to use vacuum sealed cans for coffee. Finally in 1900, RW and Austin stumbled on the system developed by the Nortons and demonstrated the power of advertising as they made vacuum packing the most popular way of packaging and merchandising our precious beans, both whole and ground.

Along came a wandering artistic Coffee advocate. Ours was a chance encounter. He was a charming young man and I must say that his creative impulses made my mother's leaves quiver. She told me a little about him, but I only know him as Briggs, the Artist. After consuming several cups of coffee, he was inspired! My mother had this affect on humans, and I must say, with all modesty, I have inherited this trait. This is not uncommon. Often, artists, after partaking of our elixir of enlightenment, are literally driven to creative moments. In this case, he was to symbolize what Coffee had done for him. Soon he was completing several sketches of a gentleman at another table in the restaurant.

His coffee inspired art involved images of an Arab gentleman wearing a flowing robe, a turban and full white beard. This gentleman was holding a cup of steaming hot coffee, and his face spoke of deep thought or mystic contemplation. Austin was inspired by what he viewed as the personification of our Ethiopian origin. Little is known of this wandering artist, or the unidentified and unknowing model who sat enjoying his coffee at another table. We do know that "The Taster" became the symbol of Hills Brothers Coffee for decades. Life-size statues drew coffee enthusiasts to their booths at trade shows, and one such statue occupied a special corner in the Hills Brothers Building in San Francisco. Atop some delivery vehicles there were smaller mechanical versions of "The Taster" forever sipping his cup of Hills Brothers Coffee.

Coffee in an instant

The turning of one century into another is a momentous event. Coffee has always enjoyed this as an opportunity to review the past hundred years and create some New Century's Eve Resolutions. Entering the 20th century was a great moment. When we reflected on the progress we had made with our last century's resolutions, it was awesome. Coffee was standing tall around the planet. In fact, we had a saying that was borrowed by the British. We used to say "The sun never sets on the Coffee Empire." We had progressed beyond all reasonable expectations with the Coffee-Human Connection. The inventive human mind, liberated and fueled by Coffee has made trains that crossed continents, making it possible to move great quantities of coffee quickly and cheaply. We had taught them how to blend and vacuum pack coffee, how to make national brands and use advertised incentives to encourage more people to partake of this elixir of wisdom.

Humans are prone to laziness, although you usually call it efficiency or progress. Regardless of what you call it, Coffee-fired imaginations devoted a great deal of time to designing and building machines to do what humans once did by hand. This included special machines to obtain the exercise you experienced by working at your physical survival. The argument was that this gave more time to drink coffee, be enlightened and be even more creative. Let's take a brief look at some of these human moments of brilliance.

Some of the greatest of the human inventions in the 19th century were in the communications arena. The typewriter was invented, along with the telegraph the telephone and camera. With faster travel, real time communication, and daily newspapers, we, the Coffees, could read the future not in tea leaves, but in the coffee grounds. We knew it was time for instant coffee. The race was on.

Satori Kato was a Japanese-American chemist, not the sidekick of the legendary Green Hornet. He was working on ways to make instant coffee that would dissolve in hot water in the 1880's. He first offered his creation to those visiting the Pan-American Exposition in 1901.

Because we had become the dominant botanical empire in the world, we were able to inspire humans in various places around the globe. The first patent for instant coffee was issued in New Zealand in 1890. David Strang developed a "dry hot air process" that he claimed had no negative affects on flavor.

Did you know George Washington invented instant coffee?

It's true. No, not the George Washington smiling at you from the dollar bill. This George W. was a coffee fanatic and inventor from Belgium. He came to the United States in 1897. His full name was George Constant Louis Washington. While he wasn't really the first to invent instant coffee, he was the first to successfully mass market it. We worked very hard with this George Washington, and through the influence we had on his creativity, called inventiveness in this industrial age, he held over 25 patents on everything from cameras and oil lamps to coffee processing. He spent some time researching Coffee in Central America.

The story we tell is about the way Coffee cleverly plants clues for the humans to find. In this case, we used a silver coffee pot. It seems that some coffee had been left in this pot, and the pot was sitting in the hot sun. The water evaporated leaving behind dried coffee residue. George took a spoon and scraped this sediment from the pot. Then, he added hot water. You talk about an AHA moment!

But the plot thickens. This George Washington's friend and doctor was Federico Lehnhoff Wyld. Dr. Wyld was also a Coffee fan, some said fanatic. Could there have been some collaboration, either intentional or accidental, or was it outright theft? We don't know, but Dr. Wyld did market the same method in Europe close to the same time George was forming the George Washington Coffee Company, and beginning to mass merchandise his instant coffee. In 1909 George began selling Red E Coffee. Isn't that a clever pun? The next year he founded the George Washington Coffee Refining Company, just in time for WWI. The War Department contracted for all the coffee he could produce. The value of coffee was deeply appreciated by the military, not only for the intellectual benefits, but because it was thought to help in recovery from mustard gas poisoning.

The soldiers referred to their coffee as a "cup of George." In a letter home from the trenches, one of the soldiers wrote *I am very happy despite the rats, the rain, the mud, the draughts, the roar of the cannon and the scream of shells. It takes only a minute to light my little oil heater and make some George Washington Coffee... Every night I offer up a special petition to the health and well-being of Mr. Washington.*

In 1943 the George Washington Coffee Company was sold to American Home Products, and George retired to dabble in real estate and drink coffee until his death at the age of 74 in 1946.

Discovering the essence of Coffee

Sometimes marketable discoveries are the result of a timely accident. At least this is the source of many of the myths and legends that you humans take such delight in. Let's go to Germany in 1820, to the lab of chemist Friedlieb Ferdinand Runge. There, one afternoon while sharing a pot of freshly brewed coffee with a friend, Johann Wolfgang von Goethe the poet, philosopher, scientist, novelist and all around creative genius. Personally, I think Herr Goethe was one of our greatest accomplishments, and a great example of what coffee can do when we devote leaf and bean to a serious goal. He is best known for the icon of enlightenment literature, *Faust*. He had a deep appreciation for the botanical world and diligently studied us to know us better. In 1790, years before any other scientist, Goethe published *Versuch die Metamorphose der Pflanzen zu erklären, (Metamorphosis of Plants)* Forgive my digression. It's just that we, the Coffees, are very proud of Herr Goethe.

Back to these two great German minds. JW had complained of insomnia and the two intellectuals pondered the possible influence of the beverage they both relied upon for their intellectual and creative inspiration. Could it be that the source of their mental powers could be the source of insomnia as well? Goethe asked Runge if it was possible to analyze the component in coffee that awakened the creativity of the human mind. Dr. Runge set to work, with a quantity of raw coffee beans and pots of strong, mind empowering German coffee. Soon he had isolated pure caffeine. He had discovered our essence!

The beans are ruined!

For some strange and unfathomable reason, as the 20th century was dawning, the drive was on to create marketable coffee without caffeine. A coffee importer and patron of the arts, Dr. Ludwig Roselius was also a bit of a scientist. I'm certain you have all heard of the clever saying credited to a rather bitter botanical luminary, the lemon. You know the old adage, "When life gives you lemons, make lemonade." It is beyond my comprehension why one would want to drink sour old lemonade when delightful coffee is available, but that's the way it is with some of you humans. Well, this book isn't about lemons, so we shall leave that subject and return to somewhat more invigorating and enlightening material. Still, this is a tale about human folly. Forgive me. I digress.

Back to Dr. Roselius. A shipment of coffee arrived in port, surviving a horrendous storm that soaked the precious cargo of green (raw) Nicaraguan coffee beans with salt water. At first they thought the cargo was ruined, but after a few cups of "good" coffee they decided to dry, roast and grind some of the damaged beans and see if they were ruined or still salable. The answer was 'yes.' But it seemed there might be something missing. This led to a couple years of intense research. The end result was that a process for removing about 97% of the caffeine and a patent in 1906. The method that seemed to work best was a combination of steam and a benzine wash. It was most effective at removing our precious caffeine, without totally destroying the flavor.

When the concept was taken to France, it was marketed as Café Sans Caffeine, or Sanka. This became the trade name in the 1920's when it arrived in America. Swiss coffee experts developed a decaffeinating method using only water, and several other methods were invented, but I still see no reason for coffee without caffeine.

There's a lot of coffee in Brazil

This story is one about "too much of a good thing." I told you earlier in this text about how we entered Brazil as a part of a romantic interlude between the wife of French Guiana's governor and the dashingly handsome diplomat and military officer, Lt. Col. Francisco de Melo Palheta.

I am reluctant to say that we thrived in Brazil in part because of the great care the coffee trees received from slave labor. This was in the early days and I am relieved to say slavery was abolished in Brazil in 1888. It was the last nation in the western hemisphere to end this horrid practice.

Brazilian Coffee production continued to increase. In fact, we were so successful in that beautiful nation that, in the 1930's, and for the next decade, there was a coffee surplus. This was, at least in part, the result of a strange course of events that took place in the United States. In January 1920, the 18th Amendment to the US Constitution took effect. This was an attempt to forbid the production, sale or consumption of alcoholic beverages. We applauded this as a giant step forward in your domestication. A boom in coffee sales resulted, as well as the creation of an underground alcohol industry in the United States. This prompted greater coffee production in Brazil, and soon she was the largest producer of coffee in the world.

Soon after the 18th Amendment was ratified, the 19th Amendment became a part of American culture. This is one of the greatest additions to the US Constitution ever. America's freed male slaves had gained the right to vote more than 50 years earlier. Finally, on August 18, 1920, American women had the right to vote. We appreciated this and hosted a nationwide coffee party to celebrate these two additions to the Constitution. The future was looking very good for Coffee. Women could now vote, and they were great coffee consumers. This meant that with the other half of the American public liberated and given voice. Progress in the enlightenment of humankind could now race ahead. New ideas, new creativity, perhaps even a decline in violence could follow.

Then our dreams were shattered. The 21st Amendment was passed in 1933. This repealed the 18th amendment and made alcoholic beverages legal again. While women continued to prefer coffee, many men returned to the consumption of all those mind befuddling beverages. This soon spelled disaster for Brazil's coffee industry. This is when Frank and *The Coffee Song* came on the global scene. But this song was only a part of the action we, the creative Coffees inspired in an attempt to salvage the Coffee-Human Connection and our investment in Brazil.

Frank Sinatra and The Coffee Song

I must admit that I have a deep affection for Frank Sinatra. What Coffee lady could resist those blue eyes of his? He truly loved coffee, and there have been family rumors about Frank and my grandmother having a little fling. As a token of gratitude he helped promote coffee with *The Coffee Song* written by Bob Hilliard and Dick Miles in 1946.

There are numerous recordings available including this one on YouTube **www.youtube.com/watch?v=H3MqmV47Lq8** and the lyrics are included later in this book on page 108.

Freeze Dried Coffee

Through the 1930's Coffee plantations and the people who tended us throughout Brazil were reeling from too much success and a decline in demand from the United States. It was so bad that some of the Brazilian locomotives were fueled with coffee beans rather than coal. The very thought of this makes my leaves shudder and my branches droop. There was even a suggestion that cargo ships be loaded with the surplus coffee and hauled out to sea and dumped; an event that would have made the Boston Tea Party a pathetic little joke. There were comments from a few of our forward thinking Coffees that it might be better to transfer the domestication project from humans to dolphins. However, this was rejected because dolphins lack opposable thumbs. I personally think there may be some potential for such a partnership. Personally, I think dolphins are kinda cute, but not nearly as cute as Juan Valdez.

After a lengthy meeting where much coffee was consumed, we were able to inspire a gathering of Brazilian politicians and the people we had selected to care for our plantations and continue the work of humankind's domestication. They decided to turn to a small but enterprising business in Switzerland. There a true intellectual fan of coffee, Max Morgenthaler, with our encouragement and support, went to work on a way to convert the bulky raw coffee beans into much more compact, long lasting coffee cubes. Finally, after several years of research and untold gallons of coffee, Max and his team developed a unique powdered coffee. This was in 1938. In the process, they developed a freeze-drying technique that preserved the flavor better. Within a couple years, production was taking place in England, France, USA, South Africa and Argentina.

World War II was on the horizon and coffee consumption was on the increase in Washington, D.C. President Roosevelt was a famous coffee consumer. And some of the Coffee family insist that it was coffee that inspired so many of the innovations that came from this city in this period, and that we charted the course of the history itself.

As preparation for war and ways to provide for the troops became serious concerns, we suggested to the military leaders that a historical precedent showed the way. After all, we initiated the American revolution in the coffeehouses and declared coffee the official beverage of the fledgling United States. During the Civil War coffee was a part of the troops' rations.

This historical wisdom was accepted, and coffee became a part of the famous (or infamous) C-Rations that sustained the American soldiers as they entered the conflict. Because weight and durability were important considerations, they used instant coffee. Because the GI's were a generous lot, they frequently shared their coffee rations with others they encountered. This dynamic coffee company from Switzerland couldn't have devised a better ad campaign. When the war was over and the soldiers came home, they brought a taste for this instant coffee with them. Today, this coffee that kept the GI's thinking is still known as Nescafé and Nestlé continues to be one of the world's leading innovators of instant coffees. They produce more than 200 special blends for regional tastes in facilities in many of the developing countries where we are grown.

Chapter 6
Juan Valdez & A Theme Park for Coffee

100% Colombian Coffee

Mickey Mouse is a famous global icon, but even Mickey is no match for the Juan Valdez, the personification of Coffee, the world's favorite beverage. Senor Valdez was given to the world by the Colombian coffee growers. I know. You are going to tell me that coffee comes in second to water, but let's face it. There is no comparison between the two. We are an institution. We are the driving force in the enlightenment and inspiration of all humankind. Water only keeps you alive. We give a reason to be alive. Forgive me. I digress.

Back in the 1920's the cafeteros , (coffee farmers), of Columbia joined together to form the Federación Nacional de Cafeteros de Colombia. If you speak English, you may know this as the National Federation of Coffee Growers of Colombia. You may not know the Federation but you certainly know their symbol. He is an exceedingly attractive man with a moustache, a white straw hat, a striped serape over his shoulder and a more pleasant than average mule named Conchita.

I have seen the little movies they play between boring segments of TV programs. These mini-information pieces show the world how Senor Valdez grows and hand picks our coffee cherries at the peak of perfection. Doesn't he have the most delightful accent though? The world refers to him as Juan Valdez, but I think of him as MY Mr. Coffee.

Would you like to know a little more about this fascinating, kind and gentle cafetero? Yes, that was a foolish question. I know you want to learn more about him. The truth is, there have been several individuals handsome enough to be selected for this role. I like to think of them as follows.

Juan Valdez # 1

It was 1958 and the National Federation of Coffee Growers of Colombia was looking for a television star. They found him in New York. His name was Jose F. Duval. He was born and raised in Havana and he had a fabulous voice.

After he arrived in the United States he starred in a production of *Die Fledermaus* at the Metropolitan Opera. As you know, this light-hearted operetta was composed by Johann Strauss II. Jose was simply stunning in the role, and it's a tribute to his monumental generosity and humility that he refused top billing. He knew that other performers needed the publicity. He had a great career in musical productions including James Michener's *South Pacific* and he starred in many movies including The *Cardinal* and *The Mambo Kings*. It had to be true love for him to give up this great singing career for Coffee. He defined the role and perfected the character we all know and love as Juan Valdez. Jose WAS Juan Valdez for a formative decade that made Columbian coffee a household word.

Juan Valdez #2

When Jose retired from the role of Juan Valdez, the Federation selected Carlos Sanchez, an artist/actor from Medellin, Colombia, who carried on the traditional role Jose had defined for a decade. In 1969 Carlos became Juan Valdez, and literally grew old as the personification of 100% Columbian coffee. Carlos was a man of the people and was often seen on those delightful TV commercials entering a stranger's kitchen when they were in need of a superior coffee. He once appeared in the White House serving coffee, and was in the movie *Bruce Almighty*.

Carlos started a chain of Juan Valdez Cafés in 2002 and these100% Columbian coffee shops can now be found around the world. Carlos gave a smiling face to Columbian coffee for 37 years. In 2006 he decided to retire and return to his home in Medellin to sip coffee and create peaceful beauty as an artist.

This caused one of the most intense searches ever. The problem would be equal to Walt Disney being faced with Mickey's retirement. How could they replace this actor/coffee icon who had become the "man on the can" of "the richest coffee in the world." The decision was a stroke of genius. Obviously, the 560,000 members of the National Federation of Coffee Growers of Colombia gained their inspiration and insight from their product. Was this where the next Juan Valdez could be found? Could he be a real Columbian cafetero?

Juan Valdez # 3

They had unexpected success with a singer from Havana and an artist/actor from Medellin. The search was on and auditions were being held throughout Columbia. Sometimes accidents happen and this was the case with Carlos Castaneda, a third generation coffee farmer from the hillside village of Andes. Before 2006 he continued a family tradition with seven and a half acres of hillside that supported about a small coffee plantation. He picked his first ripe coffee cherries when he was only six years old, and has been tenderly caring for us since.

At the age of 39, Carlos Castaneda became the third Juan Valdez. It is soooo good to have another handsome man with a twinkle in his eye and love in his heart for all of us Coffees. But, Juan was more than just a leaf throb for Coffee trees around the globe, he became the role model for what the perfect enlightened human looks and behaves like. And this Senor Castaneda continues to be the shining example.

Until he was discovered, he had never been to Bogota, never been in an airplane and lived the life of a poor farmer. But he was more than a farmer. He was a cafetero, a Coffee farmer. Sigh! My Hero!

Now, I will tell you about his accidental discovery. The story goes that one day he was in town and dropped by a local diner for a cup of coffee. There were several people in fancy clothes with big cameras in the street. "What are they doing?" he asked a friend as they shared coffee and watched the activity.

"The Federation's looking for a new Juan Valdez." His friend replied.

Just then one of the men wearing sunglasses and looking very nervous came over to their table. "Hey! You know anything about coffee?" he asked the question, but didn't wait for an answer. He turned and motioned to the lady with the camera. Soon they were pasting a moustache on his lip and putting a white straw hat on his head. While they led him to the mule standing in the shade, they carefully placed a striped serape over his shoulder.

"Conchita, meet your new Juan Valdez," the man with the sunglasses spoke sarcastically while the lady with the camera snapped about a dozen photos. She asked him a barrage of questions while giving him little time to answer. Then, smiled, wrote his name and address on a card and continued doen the street. Then he went back to his coffee and a discussion common to farmers around the world. "Been dry. Think we'll get a good rain soon? I'm a little worried about the crop this year."

All over Columbia the search continued. Finally they had narrowed the field to about 400 cafeteros. One of these finalists in this unique "Coffee's Got Talent" contest was going to be the new Juan Valdez. They were quizzed, interviewed, auditioned, analyzed by psychologists, and studied by advertising experts. He even practiced signing Juan Valdez autographs on everything from coffee bags to tee shirts, plane tickets to café menus, even napkins. The contestants had to show that they could interact with children, academics, business executives, newlyweds, reporters, politicians, world leaders, mules and, of course, us Coffee trees.

We had our eyes, and leaves, on Carlos from the start, and did everything we could to groom him for this role. We did this, not for any advantage to Coffee, but for the continued domestication of humankind, the promotion of world peace, solutions to global warming and the continued enlightenment of all humans everywhere, before it's too late. You have to understand that as the plant who domesticated humanity, we have an awesome, sometimes overwhelming, responsibility to the rest of life on Earth. As my grandmother was fond of telling the seedlings, "It ain't easy being the bean who conquered the world."

The transition took place in a well manicured coffee grove in Columbia. It was a day filled with emotion. Carlos Sanchez was retiring. He slowly walked up the path holding the reins of the faithful mule Conchita. Carlos Castaneda was coming through the coffee trees, but he wore only the shirt, tan pants, sandals and moustache. They met before the most beautiful coffee tree I have ever seen. It was in full bloom, with bright ripe berries as well as flowers. I must confess that this was the result of costuming and makeup. We don't usually flower and fruit at the same time. Oh, how I wish I could have been her. But I could never have kept my branches off either of these two Juans.

Sanchez stepped forward and removed the serape from his shoulder. "I present to you the accessories that I have used all my life," he said, as he placed it perfectly over Castaneda's shoulder. Then he did the same with his leather bag and the signature white hat. I've always wanted to know what was in that bag. Finally, symbolically transferring the reigns of power, he presented the reins of the faithful companion and trusted servant, Conchita the mule. With the cameras rolling to record this peaceful transfer of power, Conchita brayed her opinion.

We had reached the point where the sun never set on the coffee empire. Coffee plants were waving their leafy arms to the sun and coffee drinkers were greeting the day with a steaming cup of the elixir of morning somewhere on the earth every minute of the day. Our hard work and dedication were beginning to pay off. We were moving ever closer to the ultimate achievement, something no member of the plant kingdom has ever achieved. Oh sure. Many insects have been trained and conditioned to serve a specific isolated plant. The Myrmecophytes are a good example of this. These are plants that provide food and housing for pitiful little colonies of a few species of ants. These little creatures then defend, pollinate, and groom these plants. But this is hardly the magnitude we Coffees attempted.

I know. You are going to tell me about the eucalyptus and those funny looking, cuddly koalas. How can you possibly compare that dull old marsupial to the intellectual pinnacle of the animal kingdom? Besides, I don't think you could convince any Coffee tree that koalas are even close to Juan Valdez in ultimate cuteness. And Juan has repaid our efforts the same way Mickey rewarded Walter Elias Disney, with an amusement park.

The National Coffee Park (Parque Nacional del Café)

Yes, it's true. In 1995 the National Federation of Coffee Growers of Colombia created a Coffee inspired version of Disneyland. This is a massive theme park located in Quindío, Colombia. I like to think of this as an educational institution. It's part botanical garden and part theme park. You can enjoy the thrill rides, but there are also restaurants, music, souvenir shops, animated flowers and photo opportunities at every turn. That handsome, kind, compassionate and brilliant Juan Valdez wanders the park greeting fans and signing autographs.

This Parque Nacional del Café is in two parts, with gondola lifts. There are over two dozen attractions, not counting Juan Valdez. These include the interactive museum and exhibits taking you on a grand historical coffee tour. There are great exhibits showing you how to grow, harvest, process and package coffee. You even have an opportunity to purchase some before you leave for the day. The "Coffee Show" is a coffee ballet with coffee inspired song and dance. Guided tours and horseback riding trails take you through perhaps the most compete presentation of live and growing coffee varieties in the world. This is a real working coffee plantation. Nearby is a bamboo forest and striking plantings and colorful flowers abound.

In the valley beyond are the thrill rides and amusements, including a traditional train ride with live music and other entertainments. The La Broca Roller Coaster was actually moved from the Worlds of Fun Amusement Park in Kansas City, MO. A Ferris Wheel, dodge'ms, a log flume, go-carts and bumper boats are only part of the thrill ride opportunities for visitors. You are encouraged to see the educational exhibits, stroll through the coffee plantation, dine on the good food and enjoy the great coffee. You might even get Juan's autograph, if you're lucky.

1972 Joltin' Joe and Mr. Coffee

This was a ground breaking moment in coffee history. The first automatic drip home coffee maker, with the formal name of Mr. Coffee, was introduced by Cleveland, Ohio entrepreneur Vincent Marotta. Juan Valdez will always be my Mr. Coffee, but, this innovation did revolutionize both home and office coffee making. Water is percolated through the coffee grounds at 200° Fahrenheit, as opposed to the boiling water that flowed through grounds in the old-fashioned percolator, and the even older coffee pot.

Mr. Coffee soon became a household name because it was pitched on TV by the legendary baseball great and Hall of Fame recipient Joe DiMaggio. In the late 1970's 40,000 units a day were sold. It still is the world's best-selling coffee maker for home use, even though there are literally hundreds of brands and models on the store shelves today. There is a new challenge as well. The single-serve Keurig system is making inroads. I shall share more information on innovation later.

Chapter 7
From the Age of Aquarius
to the Age of Coffee

Some may consider the Coffee-Human Connection akin to a drug addiction, while others like to think of this as almost a religion, but it's really a very long term love affair. This is a relationship where both us, the Coffees, and you, the humans have gained so much. Isn't this the essence of a good healthy relationship? We have inspired you humans in so many ways. We powered your intellect, your curiosity and your sense of adventure, first to new continents and new concepts like mathematics and democracy.

You, in turn, have taken us around this great planet we both call home, and helped us take root everywhere. But you have also been inspired by us to seek new and better ways to celebrate our partnership, from the coffee ceremonies of Ethiopia to the penny universities of London, campfires where stories and coffee were shared, to customs like coffee breaks and theme parks devoted to us.

We inspired you to journey to the moon, and you took us with you. The first coffee sipped on the moon was a part of the meal consumed by astronauts Neil Armstrong and Buzz Aldrin before they went for a walk. Their meal included bacon, sugar cookies, peaches and pineapple-grapefruit juice, but the most important part of their "out of this world meal" was the coffee. This coffee break was enjoyed before their historic moonwalk on July 20, 1969. Thank you Neil and Buzz for taking us to the moon with you.

I have it on good authority that Neil's first words on landing were in response to Buzz's suggestion that they go for a walk. Neil's historic comment was not about their footprints, but rather a matter of establishing priorities. "Yes, Buzz, we'll go for a walk, but first we have coffee." was what Neil is rumored to have said.

For the Love of Peet

You humans sought to improve this relationship with a parade of inventions ranging from the coffee pot to the percolator, Mr. Coffee to Keurig. Some were inspired by a sincere desire to improve our intimate relationship with you. Others were driven only by greed. Innovation in the coffee industry has been so dynamic that today we are second only to oil in commodity trading. Oil may fuel your machines, but our work is far more important. We fuel the human mind.

For this reason many humans not only view coffee consumption as a religious experience, they also dutifully visit the temples and chapels where they can meditate over their morning inspirational message. For many, these religious experiences take place in independent coffeehouses, while others are inclined to visit the chain chapels where they can even receive a drive-through inspirational message.

What happens when two teachers and a writer team up to create a new concept in coffee shops? The largest global chain of coffee chapels is, of course, Starbucks. This Starbucks story begins with a Dutch coffee trader, Alfred Peet. He moved to America after World War II. He hadn't intended to start a coffee revolution. He just disliked the style of coffee served in the US. In 1966 he opened Peet's Coffee & Tea store on the corner of Walnut and Vine Streets in Berkeley, CA. There he sold not only cups of well-brewed coffee, but fresh roasted ground coffee for discriminating tastes. You humans failed to notice that another revolution was brewing.

Within three years Peet's Coffee House became a magnet for devoted followers of quality coffee. These followers became known as Peetniks, and the area became home to a number of local food enthusiasts. This became known as the Gourmet Ghetto and some call it the birthplace of the artisan coffee movement. While many consider Seattle the epicenter of coffee innovation, we like to think of Berkeley as Coffee's Mecca. It was here that three teachers and a writer became adherents of a new style of coffee, and coffee service.

The Starbucks Founders

It's only proper that literate types be inspired to spread the word about the value of coffee over other mundane beverages. Jerry Baldwin was an English teacher and Zev Seigel taught history, while Gordon Bowker was a coffee inspired writer before his conversion to coffee entrepreneur. These three wise men opened the first Starbucks storefront in Seattle, Washington in 1971. They did this with less than ten thousand dollars in start-up capital. Zev worked at Peets in Berkeley for several months to learn the basics of quality coffee making. With Alfred's encouragement, this trio patterned their coffee house after Peet's in Berkeley. Of course they purchased their coffee beans from Alfred for the first year or so.

Less than a decade later, they had six locations in Seattle and were purchasing coffee directly from selected growers. They continued to be a local coffee house chain until 1982 when Howard Schultz, a salesman working for a Swedish supplier entered the picture. Jerry Baldwin was impressed with his skill as a salesman and soon hired him as the director of marketing for the fledgling Starbucks chain. Schultz was intrigued with the café culture he had encountered in Italy where he tasted his first latte and espresso.

The rest is history, our history and yours. The Starbucks folks want to think they own us now, but they are only following through with what we Coffees inspired them to develop. They are totally dependant on us. Think about this. Where would Starbucks be without Coffee? Regardless, they have taken coffee in new directions and encouraged coffee consumption in other parts of the globe. The first Starbucks beyond US borders was opened in Tokyo in 1996, and they invaded Britain in 1998.

You like to think of this as a new innovation, but what was really the basis for Starbucks success was the reinvention of the European coffeehouse with specially prepared and finely served styles of coffee. It was not an easy journey. Schultz had a difficult time convincing Baldwin of the virtues of these fancy "old world" styles of coffee, and was less than enthusiastic about the idea of an espresso bar in a Starbucks. Schultz was convinced that he was right, and in 1985 he left Starbucks.

In 1987, Schultz raised enough capital with local investors to purchase Starbucks from Jerry Baldwin and Gordon Bowker. One of these backers was a guy named Bill Gates, whose son, Bill Gates Junior, also did pretty well for himself in the Seattle area. Incidentally, both Gates have a strong affection for coffee.

This was a concept that soon grew beyond Seattle. Like Coffee's global empire, the sun never sets on the Starbucks empire either. In 1987 there were 17 Starbucks. By 2000 there were 3,501 stores with new stores opening in Australia, Hong Kong and a number of countries in the middle east including Saudi Arabia and the United Arab Emirates. In 2012 17,651 Starbucks stores could be found in more than 60 countries. As the spokesplant for all Coffees everywhere, I must say we are very appreciative of the great work Starbucks has done for not only Coffee, but the growers with the concepts of fair trade and grower cooperatives. They have also been active with the environment, by encouraging organic and sustainable coffee production.

However, there is one little problem I have with Starbucks. That is their logo. While we tried to inspire the use of our beautiful flowers, or a handful of our bright red cherries, or even some roasted seeds, these three 'wise guys' collective minds were obviously somewhere else. They adapted an old 15th century Norse woodcut depicting a half naked siren from Greek mythology. Did they really think this vulgarly posed twin-tailed mermaid with bare breasts uncombed hair was more attractive to coffee drinkers than the beauty of my flowers, or the caress of my leaves?

It even gets worse. Let's look at this siren's intentions. Her evil goal was to seduce the sailors who had been at sea for an extended time. The myth says it was her beautiful voice that lured these poor men to their untimely end. I'm not so sure it was her voice that was so irresistible.

Why this Coffee inspired , educated and creative trio have chosen this indecently exposed woman, who was half fish and lacked any indication of an ability to carry on an intelligent conversation is beyond me. Is this really an appropriate logo of a global Coffee empire? It implies that we have a great deal of work yet to do, before you are truly domesticated.

When Mr. Schultz purchased Starbucks in 1987, he had the decency to clean up this disgusting logo a bit. Her bare breasts were covered by her rather disheveled hair, and the color was changed from that dull brown to a far more attractive green inspired by our beautiful leaves. The words on this logo were reduced to *Starbucks Coffee*. Rather than the original *Starbucks - Coffee - Tea - Spices* on what looked like a low budget cigar band.

In 2011, in celebration of the 40th anniversary of Starbucks, they again changed the logo. They combed the stupid siren's hair and eliminated all words. I doubt she could read anyway. At least they kept the beautiful leaf green color. I have been working with them to change the fish tails to coffee leaves, get the siren some makeup and put a cup of coffee to her lips.

I personally think this would be much better for marketing, at least to wary sailors who know the siren myth.

Thinking small, from Singlebrew to Keurig

While the Starbucks people were thinking BIG, We Coffees were trying to find answers to the diverse needs of our domesticated humans. Sometimes it's difficult to get you humans to think small, but this is what we felt was needed. We encouraged this effort in two different directions. Actually, it was two different mountains.

Let's start with a camping trip in the magnificent Colorado Rockies in the early 1980's. Randy Schoonauer, a really serious coffee fanatic, was backpacking with some friends. We had introduced them to the joys of gourmet coffee, and they were toting all the cookware necessary to produce the perfect cup of coffee up the mountain with them. They had the coffee hot, when a minor mishap dumped the coffee, the pot and all of the extensive array of equipment either into the fire or over the side of the mountain. It always amazes me how even the aroma of coffee brewing can spark the human imagination, and inspire you humans to ever greater mental heights. This caffeine sparked genius thought "What if we put fine, freshly ground and properly roasted coffee in a tea-type bag? Then, all we would need to do is heat the water."

When he gave voice to this burst of genius, his companions became as enthusiastic as he was. "Each of us could make the coffee as dark and rich as we wanted."

Upon his return from the mountain, we Coffees fueled his mental fires and inspired him to research the coffee trade journals, consult with coffee experts and conduct marketing studies. Finally he was ready to begin testing different coffee varieties, seeking the optimum roast and grind combinations. He wanted to create a truly gourmet cup of coffee, one single brew serving at a time, prepared either in a cup in the microwave or with a pot of boiling water over a campfire. His dream was to have single brew packs like a tea bag so that everyone in a group could make a cup of their favorite coffee.

With the aid of Coffee, ideas become realities. In a few short years he launched Singlebrew which became the first 100% ground gourmet coffee in North America to be put in an individual brewing packet similar to the old fashioned tea bag. Since its inception, this single serving coffee process has expanded from 2 to 10 varieties. All you need is a microwave or boiling water and your favorite mug. The website is **www.singlebrew.com**

I must admit that Randy is one of the humans who makes my leaves flutter. I like to think of the innovation he created, with our inspiration, as the Zen of Coffee, simplicity leading to a state of awareness.

Now let's move to the Northeast, to Vermont and the Green Mountain Coffee Roasters. The Green Mountains are beautiful and provide the backdrop of many Vermont communities including Waitsfield. In 1980 a gentleman was passing through and stopped for a cup of coffee in this little New England town. His name was Bob Stiller, and a year later the Green Mountain Coffee Roasters Company was incorporated. They soon moved to Waterbury where they had more room to grow. We worked with Bob, but we also seized the opportunity to inspire the staff as well. Soon they were focusing on organic coffees and fair trade sources of supply. These Green Mountain people were truly inspired. Then they encountered Keurig.

Peter Dragone and John Sylvan developed a different method for brewing single cups of coffee. They began their quest in 1990, and eight years later they launched an expensive and technically complex machine that could, if all the stars were aligned and you uttered the mantra properly, produce a single cup of coffee for each of the long line of people waiting to celebrate their coffee break. This early machine was designed for the office, but in a few years they developed a model that was suitable for home use.

The genius with this system was the miniature plastic container with a built-in filter filled with carefully roasted and ground coffee. All this was sealed in for assured freshness. The machine would puncture the top and bottom, then force just enough hot water through the K-cup, as they called it to fill your favorite coffee mug. Agreed, this was not a biodegradable mini coffee pack, but it did provide empowerment for the coffee drinker because there were special brands, blends and flavors marketed, all for you to choose from. Keurig became the property of the Green Mountain Coffee Roasters in 2006, and history continues to be made with a do-it-yourself system some complain makes the coffeehouse a bargain, but it can't be beat for convenience.

Those great folks at Green Mountain have even created the Cafe Express, a coffee club for their fans. I was seriously considering starting a "Lady Coffee Fan Club" myself, but I am far too modest. Perhaps you readers will seize the opportunity.

Back to the Green Mountain Boys. We know some of you humans are concerned with the complexity of the machines required to use the K-cups but we have always encouraged you to develop and use technology.

Some have complained that these K-cups aren't environmentally friendly. Let's be patient. It could be said that humans are often not always eco-friendly either. We do understand that you must be considered a work in progress and we have a long way to go with your ultimate enlightenment. I must confess that we also have a lot to learn about you humans.

Part II
Coffee Inspired Cultures

Chapter 8
Coffee in Ritual and Ceremony

Communion of the Coffee Cup
by Tomi Jill Folk

Dad was one step closer to heaven
with each good-bye he said.
And each day and passing hour
He spent more time in bed.
But when each of his precious family
Came home to bid him well
He mustered up the strength somehow
to hear what they would tell,
And share a cup of coffee,
Perhaps a sip or two,
Then when most of us departed,
His time on Earth was through.

As first spring breezes blow this year,
Upon Dad's birthday eve,
He celebrates with those who've gone before,
His heavenly gift received.

This was written by my editor/publisher Tomi Jill Folk about her father's last days. He was a great friend of all Coffees, a gentle man and a great gardener. He understood that coffee was for sharing, and this informal ritual spent enjoying the beverage and the conversation symbolized the way in which he cherished his family. Tomi wrote this tribute on March 20, 2007, which would have been her father's 79th birthday. She wrote it at 41,000 feet in altitude, on her way to Florida for his memorial service.

Coffee culture: Coffee as sacrament

Coffee has a long history as a spiritual substance. Frederick Wellman, in his book *Coffee: Botany, Cultivation, and Utilization*, describes an African blood-brother ceremony in which the blood of the two individuals is mixed and put between the twin seeds of a coffee fruit, then swallowed.

Coffee was first used as a snack, then as medicine. But it soon became a part of religious observances, a part of prayer ritual and meditation both in solitude and in groups. Pilgrims to Mecca carried coffee all over the Moslem world. Some early Christians viewed coffee as the bitter invention of Satan. They actually favored wines, beers and ales for religious worship and ceremony. Still, it rapidly became a part of the ritual of pot luck socials and pancake dinners, even those long boring meetings after some church services.

Coffee ceremonies

For people in the Horn of Africa and parts of the Middle East, coffee has maintained its religious connotations, and the ritual aspects remain conscious and refined. Ethiopians and Eritreans brought their coffee ceremonies with them as they immigrated to the United States. My literary collaborators Tomi and Hank first experienced this formal coffee ceremony as guests of a new found Eritrean friend met at EPCOT.

Being invited to an Ethiopian or Eritrean coffee ceremony is considered an honor, and the procedure can take upwards of two delightful hours.

The Eritrean hostess carefully roasted the green (raw) coffee beans in a shallow pan, and passed the just-roasted, steaming beans around the small room so that everyone could enjoy the delightful aroma. Then she cooled them on a small straw mat. Next she ground them with mortar and pestle. This ground coffee was slowly stirred into a clay coffee pot she called the *jebena*. It had a rounded bottom and sat on a wire stand over a small flame.

This potent, caffeine enriched beverage was served in small china cups. She poured the brew into the cups from a height of a foot or more and never spilled a drop. Next she added several spoons of sugar and stirred lightly. The coffee was strong but not bitter. She explained to us novices that it was to be savored in small sips. The entire event was an opportunity to talk and share stories while watching the preparation of the beverage. For Tomi and Hank this was a delightful and most memorable experience, a ritual designed to make them feel welcome, but it was also an opportunity for some friendly and intelligent conversation.

The chief steward, or *kahveghi*

We Coffees have a special place in our leaves for the place you call Turkey. It has long been world famous for both the ways it honors and serves Coffee. The people there have some great coffee traditions and rituals. In ancient Turkey, wealthy families often had a special member of the household staff, called the *kahveghi*, whose sole responsibility was to attend to the preparation and service of coffee. Sometimes referred to as the chief steward, this kahveghi, was provided special quarters next to the room where guests were served both coffee and conversation. Beautiful furnishings and a special array of more coffee accouterments than your average Viennese coffeehouse, made this room magnificent. While the coffee was being consumed and both host and guests were being energized by the coffee, conversation and ideas flowed. I have read that the coffee was served in special coffee dishes that were only half filled so that it could be held with the thumb on the bottom and the two fingers on the upper edge.

Coffee Rituals around the world

Today a multitude of coffee ceremonies can be found all around the world: in office lunchrooms, in espresso bars, in Swedish parlors, in Japanese coffeehouses, wherever coffee drinkers gather to stare into space, to read a newspaper, or to share a moment with their friends without obligation. These rituals are a sensory celebration that involves aroma as much as flavor, ambiance and decor, service and guests. The ritual and ceremony of Coffee is varied and finds delightfully unique and diverse expression. The colors, flavors, scents and sounds can be a part of the setting, furniture, service, utensils, gestures and attitude. Sounds combine to establish a sense of comfort and a mood of contemplation or well-being. This can go far beyond music. Some of my more mature fellow Coffees contend that this is the reason for popularity of the percolator in post WWII American culture. I think it sounds like an old John Deere tractor. I must admit that I do kinda like the old Ventures instrumental *Percolator* on their Telstar album way back in 1963. I think it was adapted from an even earlier Maxwell House Coffee TV ad.

There is a froth that forms in the pot when coffee is brewing. For people of the Middle East and parts of Europe, this foam is an important part of the drink. It's more than a matter of flavor. This froth serves as a focus for the meditative aspects of sharing coffee, or seeking inspiration in solitude. Not only does it taste good, it symbolizes the meditative glow that can occur when both brewing and consuming coffee. Espresso became popular in Italy and we have encouraged its appreciation around the world. In coffeehouses everywhere, this "crema" as it is called, is a key part of not only espresso, but caffe latte and cappuccino as well. This froth possesses a subtle flavor, but for the true coffee connoisseur it is the texture that provides the allure and the sensory experience. It has become a medium for coffee artists around the world. Coffee people are so creative. This is one of best qualities of you humans. There are excellent videos on YouTube showing actual coffee artists creating their momentary works.

Sometimes we forget that the preparation of a fine cup of coffee is a work of art and whether it's you, in your own home, or a professional in a fine coffee house, coffee is worthy of respect as an art form.

Reading the coffee grounds

Long ago we Coffees worked with the women in Turkey to develop what has become a tradition in many of the Armenian and Turkish coffee houses today. For the reading to be accurate, it is best to use an expert we have worked with for years. This resident 'reader,' is usually a grandmotherly type, skilled in the ritual and knowledgeable in the interpretation of the grounds remaining in the coffee cup.

As is the case with most coffee rituals, it can only be valid if the coffee was prepared properly and your consumption was done slowly, with meditation and adherence to the ritual itself. Warning, this coffee is strong and should only be consumed in small sips, then savored before swallowing.

For many readers, it is important that you drink from only one side of the cup. This will vary with the location and the individual reader. This is from one such ceremony, but they do vary considerably. When only the grounds remain, she will sit with you and coach you through a series of steps.
1. You will place the saucer on top of the cup, and she will make some motions above the saucer, usually with a short prayer or incantation.
2. Next, she will take the saucer and cup from your hands and carefully turn them over as she places them on the table.
3. If you are seeking money, this is the time to place a coin on top of the inverted cup. Conversation will follow as the cup cools, and the grounds slowly form their message.
4. The coffee reader will open the cup. This means separating the cup and the saucer, sometimes with special movements and comments. The grounds will form different patterns around the inside and bottom of the cup. This is where the skill of the reader comes in. She will point out and interpret the images. These will often be more reminiscent of some of Jackson Pollock's abstract

expressionist art. I think Coffee may have been a primary influence on his creativity.

5. From the conversation while you were waiting for the coffee to cool, she will know what insights you are seeking and will be attuned to those issues.

6. Occasionally, there will be a continuation of the reading with the grounds on the saucer.

An English magazine from 1731 contained an account of divination by coffee-grounds. The writer made the following comments. *Surprised the lady and her company in close cabal over their coffee, the interest very intent upon one whom, by her address and intelligence, he guessed was a tire woman* [a lady's maid], *to which she added the secret of divining by coffee grounds. She was then in full inspiration, and with much solemnity observing the atoms around the cup; on the one hand sat a widow, on the other a maiden lady. They assured me that every cast of the cup is a picture of all one's life to come, and every transaction and circumstance is delineated with the exactest certainty.*

I find the advertisement used by this seer is quite interesting. I wonder how a TV commercial would promote the same skills.

An advise is hereby given that there has lately arrived in this city (Dublin) the famous Mrs. Cherry, the only gentlewoman truly learned in the occult science of tossing of coffee grounds; who has with uninterrupted success for some time past practiced to the general satisfaction of her female visitants. Her hours are after prayers are done at St. Peter's Church, until dinner.

She never requires more than 1 oz. of coffee from a single gentlewoman, and so proportioned for a second or third person, but not to exceed that number at any one time.

If the one ounce of coffee represented her payment for reading the future, the charge could not be considered exorbitant!

Yatehay (Ya'ah'tee)

This is the traditional Navajo greeting and it means "the universe is good" and is spoken to welcome someone and a part of the Navajo tradition is to follow this greeting with a cup of hot coffee. When we Coffees were introduced to the Navajo people, it was love at first sight, or should I say taste? Whenever you go into a home of a Navajo, hot coffee is always offered. That's their way of welcoming you. They are so kind to include us in this tradition.

This is how one Navajo student described the first encounter with Coffee. "When hard coffee [beans] came into Navajoland, the Navajo's didn't know how to boil it, because the coffee was hard like a rock. But somehow they found out that they had to grind the coffee first, and then boil it. Nowdays coffee is already ground when it is bought. All you have to do is pour water into the coffee pot, and then add 1/3 cup of coffee to each cup of water. After it has boiled, your coffee is done."

As they share coffee they are also inspired. We are very pleased with how the Navajo have become so creative because they enjoy the Coffee-Human Connection so much. I am thankful to my good friend Alvin Rafelito for sharing this information from an awesome Navajo high school publication.

The coffee break

While you American humans think you invented the ritual of the coffee break in the very early 20th century, I have to tell you that we had encouraged humans to pause in your daily activities for a cup or two of coffee, mid morning and mid afternoon in many other parts of the world throughout our history together. We knew that when humans take a little break from their labors to relax, converse and be invigorated by a little coffee, your attitude improves and so does your productivity.

In the early1900's several companies began offering their workers a short break. During WWII many factories provided these breaks as a token of appreciation for the united war effort. After the war was over, many workers wanted the custom to continue. Some point to 1952 as the first contract between industry and organized labor to formalize this concept. Others claim it was in 1964. Regardless, numerous studies have shown that the ritual coffee break improves attitude and productivity, particularly among the more intelligent of the employees.

This has been modified and refined to the point where many employers provide a coffee shop and make the coffee break a profitable venture. Some of the above mentioned scientific studies have concluded that the productivity increases greatly exceeded the minimal cost of providing coffee and a few minutes of "adult recess."

The coffeehouse & coffee culture today

The customs of coffeehouse and café appear to be intimately connected with the effect of coffee and caffeine on the human mind and body. Coffee stimulates conscious mental associations, whereas alcohol minimizes and stupefies. It has been said by wiser Coffees than I that consumption of alcohol invites instinctual responses involving loss of self control. This may lead to excessive aggression, anger, sex, and decline in mental function. Coffee, on the other hand, encourages you to think, talk, read, write, or contemplate romance. It is curious that the early coffee drinkers valued their coffee as *the wine of Apollo, the beverage of thought, dream, and dialectic*, and *the milk of thinkers and chess players.*

From the first coffeehouses into the present, they have been the gathering place of those who would rather talk and read, than argue or boast; rather play chess than cards, and listen contemplatively to music rather than vulgar song. The café usually opens to the street and sun, unlike bars or saloons, whose dark interiors protect the drinker from the encroachment of the sober, workaday world. The coffee drinker wants a comfortable corner in which to read a book on her kindle, observe the world on the facebook page, or simply enjoy the diversity of life parading past the window.

The café is often connected with the beginning of the workday. A customer buried in reading matter is a common sight in even the most mundane café, or a fast food restaurant that serves morning coffee. Coffeehouses throughout history, from the Turkish schools for the wise, to the English penny universities, to today's drive through coffee shops, have not been a refuge, but rather a launching pad. Writer groups and book clubs meet in today's coffee houses. The art from local artists hangs on the walls. Live music and poetry slams are a frequent part of the coffeehouse scene.

Campus life as a part of the coffee culture

I simply love college students. They are so enthusiastic and filled with both idealism and coffee. Most of them are working hard, studying long hours and still they are seeking inspiration in the sharing of coffee as a social opportunity.

One study concluded that the college student drinks an average of 20 to 30 gallons of coffee per year. That, dear readers, is a lot of coffee. Some are alarmed and call this an addiction, I am not the least bit alarmed. We Coffees expect this to be the case. Isn't this a part of the grand tradition of people gathering to share wisdom and be enlightened with the aid of coffee? I think this goes back to the concept of the Schools for the Wise in the Arab cultures of a millennia ago, and the Coffeehouses of Europe a few centuries past.

An extensive study was done as to why students would drink coffee and the findings revealed what we Coffees would have thought was the obvious. Coffee drinkers have an advantage in being able to stay awake, focus while studying and be alert during testing. The student culture also uses coffee as a socialization tool that has many benefits over the wanton consumption of spoiled grains or grapes. One factor that this study failed to explain is that coffee is also far less expensive than alcoholic beverages.

As a part of the campus culture, an average of over 75% of the students and 90% of the faculty consume coffee on a regular basis. I was pleased to see that coffee is the preferred beverage of most college chess teams and honor students. It was also interesting that more female students preferred coffee, while male students often consumed carbonated beverages that also contained caffeine.

Chapter 9
There Is No Substitute for Coffee

Because coffee is the beverage of choice for most of earth's humans, there have frequently been attempts to produce cheap and pathetically inferior substitutes for this elixir of our delightfully flavored and stimulating seeds. As the spokesplant for all the Coffees growing today, and to honor the memory of all Coffees who have grown before, I am forced to speak out.

First let me clarify something that you, as a Coffee inspired human, should already know. If you soak leaves in hot water, you are making tea. Some teas are pleasantly flavored and, if properly prepared and consumed, they can sooth, calm and transport you into a state of lethargy.

This is the opposite of the enlightenment, intellectual inspiration and creative energy that we, the world's Coffees provide as our gift to humankind. Proof of this is found in statistical facts. Few books were produced before we began working with humans on a grander scale. Travel was by foot, yours or the feet of assorted beasts. Tea, and it saddens me to say this about a fellow plant, but it is true, tea views its mission as merely to pacify, calm and limit creative passion. There is a little known exception which I mentioned earlier in this comprehensive text. I am referring to Coffee Leaf Tea. Our leaves have caffeine as well as our seeds.

Some humans have become addicted to the effects spoiled and fermented fruits such as grapes, or grains, or even roots such as potatoes, have on human behavior. It is so sad to see so many of the humans we have worked so hard to domesticate behaving so badly after consuming these fermented and distilled liquids. I can't even bring myself to call these foul drinks "beverages." They neither calm nor do they inspire. They stupify, impair reason and lead to improper behavior that NEVER happens with coffee. No one has ever been the cause of an automobile accident for Driving While Under the Influence of Coffee.

Still, other humans have become enamored of the processed seeds of a tropical weed tree called cacao. I must confess that, even as the self-appointed spokesplant for all Coffee, I have certain feelings for some of the drinks produced from these, shall I say it, also delightful seeds. In fact, and this must remain a secret between you and me, I have actually been in a relationship with Mr. Theo Broma. My leaves quiver and I blush at the very thought of him. I consider him my "Hot Chocolate." Together we made a most delightful drink many considered a most inspiring beverage. We called this awesome blending of the very essence of our existence "Café Mocha." This does not refer to the community of Mocha in Yemen where a rich flavored coffee bean is produced. This Mocha is an almost espresso with the combined essence of Theo's chocolate and my full bodied allure. Most of our better houses of Coffee enlightenment have been taught the ritual production of what I like to think of as one of the premier Coffee delights.

I should also explain that the seeds of this delightful tree are also made into pieces of candy, breakfast cereals ranging from Cocowheats to Chocolate Cheerios, even cookies and cakes. Because there is a tendency for the fruit of this weed to make humans feel good, sometimes too good, care should be taken to exercise self control and maintain propriety, if possible. Again, I must confess that sometimes even I have adapted a dangerous attitude, telling myself, "Propriety be damned." Again, this is a healthy combination because when you humans consume coffee, you are inspired to become creative, and the chocolate can provide delightful directions for your creativity. There is a reason humans call chocolate cake Devil's Food.

Then we come to the lessor drinks. These are failed attempts at producing viable substitutes when real, authentic, genuine coffee wasn't available. Many of these substitutes were drawn from the pantry. I will quote one of my relatives, a store brand Coffee, who is insulted by the substitutes and additives that bear no resemblance to real coffee. This is what she said. "Now listen up. I'm here to tell ya, if you're gonna make a drink outa sweet potatoes, peas, peanuts, carrot roots, beets, rice or barley, you ain't makin' coffee. You're makin' really thin vegetable soup."

Yet, through the ages, when faced with desperate times, you humans can commit desperate acts. I have never personally seen any of these, but I have been told by reliable sources that the following have been used when our invigorating and energizing beans weren't available. The worst must have been moldy or dried bread crusts, old biscuits, hardtack, crackers and in one reference, stale oatmeal cookies. Those unsavory leftovers were crumbled and toasted in a skillet until burnt. Then these cinders were dumped into the coffee pot with water and put on the stove or campfire to boil. In many cases an egg was added. As it cooked, the egg would sink to the bottom of the pot, collecting all these crumbs in the process, leaving only the boiled essence of burned bread. This was sometimes referred to as crumb coffee. Although, I can think of other terms that are certainly more appropriate, but less printable.

Grains, including wheat, corn, rye, rice, millet, sorghum or oats were parched, sometimes with butter or lard. Then, they were ground and dumped into the pot. The results were little better that crumb coffee. Dried beans, peanuts, cowpeas, chestnuts and acorns were also roasted, ground and tossed nto the pot designed for coffee. Peanut coffee called for ½ cup peanuts, ½ cup wheat or rye and ½ cup cow peas. This undignified mixture was then roasted to a coffee brown and ground in a hand cranked coffee mill. This was a most disgusting thing to do with a machine we helped you humans design to produce a more perfect cup of coffee.

You may call it Sweet Potato Coffee if you choose, but I still think it's vegetable soup. Hank, my research assistant, actually found a recipe printed in the Albany Patriot newspaper on Dec. 12, 1861. The following is a part of the blueprint for that culinary disaster. "Peel your sweet potatoes and slice them rather thin; dry them in the air or on a stove; then cut into pieces small enough to go into the coffee mill, then grind it. Two tablespoons full of ground coffee and three or four of ground potatoes will make eight or nine cups of coffee, clear, pure and well tasted."

Hank actually tried this and it was, in his own words, "Yuck!" So he added some onions, green peppers, corn and celery and made what he called, "an interesting soup." I later saw him feeding it to Shadow, his cute little dog, but Shadow, being quite intelligent, sniffed it, then promptly turned and walked away.

In both the North and the South during the Civil War, the fruit of the persimmon ('simmon) tree was commonly available. The large seeds were often used as buttons on the soldiers' uniforms. These seeds were also roasted, then ground and either used in place of real coffee, or used to adulterate the real thing. There was a lot of other stuff mixed with coffee because the demand so far exceeded the supply. I assure you, I do not approve of Coffee adultery, or its illegitimate offspring.

One common plant was so good as a coffee additive that it's still used today. You humans call it chicory, coffee weed, cornflower, wild endive, blue sailors and a lot of other names as well. The roots can be dried, roasted and ground. When mixed with real coffee, some humans like the flavor, although it isn't as enlightening and empowering as my elixir. Some of my human friends have told me that the delightful yellow wildflower you know as the dandelion also produces roots that can make both a delicious vegetable and a delightful coffee additive. I guess, if you must engage in adultery with your coffee, it might as well have a pretty face, and I like to think of the dandelion as a drop of golden sunshine.

The seeds of watermelons, pumpkins, squash and even sunflowers have also been used as additives, but the resulting flavor is always far from acceptable.

There was a substitute developed by C. W. Post in 1895. He formed the Postum Cereal Company to produce what he marketed as a caffeine free alternative to coffee. Postum was made from wheat bran, wheat, molasses and maltodextrin. This mixture was roasted and ground to resemble coffee. Until 1912 it was brewed much as you would real coffee. This was popular with religious communities that were reluctant to use real coffee. Later Instant Postum was developed. He even produced a special blend he called 'Coffee Flavored Postum.'

Mr. Post wasn't content to make coffee substitutes. In 1897 he put his substitute for grapes on the grocery shelves. You know this as Post Grape Nuts. Postum is still available and can be found on many grocery store shelves. But not in your neighborhood coffeehouse.

Chapter 10
To Your Health

Nutrition in your coffee cup

Thousands of years ago we, the Coffees of the World, embarked on perhaps the noblest effort ever attempted by any member of the plant kingdom. There are many altruistic and caring plants out there willing to make the ultimate sacrifice to feed your bodies, promote better health, provide clothing, tools and shelter, even musical instruments. We chose a different goal. We devoted our energy to empowering your mind and imagination, fueling your creativity and leading you to higher ground. I must admit that the higher ground thing was sometimes to bring you to the elevations where we grow, blossom and fruit best.

You may not think of your morning cup(s) of coffee as a healthy drink. In fact there is a certain thrill in considering it a bit unsavory, perhaps even unhealthy behavior because if we were honest, we would all agree that sin can be fun. It is only logical then to conclude that Coffee must somehow be sinful, because we certainly are fun.

I hesitate to break the news to you, but that cup of coffee has nutritional value. We aren't just a pretty face, and there's a lot more to us than caffeine. Recent scientific research is confirming what we have been telling you for thousands of years. We are GOOD for you!

Let's take a look at what a great source of information, the Nutritional Data website at **http://nutritiondata.self.com/facts/beverages/3898/2** has to say.

Vitamins in coffee (in 1 cup, 8 oz)

Vitamin K	0.2mcg	0%
Thiamin	0.0mg	2%
Riboflavin	0.2mg	11%
Niacin	0.5mg	2%
Folate	4.7mcg	1%
Pantothenic Acid	0.6mg	6%
Choline	6.2mg	?

Minerals in coffee 1 cup of coffee (8 oz)

Calcium	4.7mg	0%
Magnesium	7.1mg	2%
Phosphorus	7.1mg	1%

Potassium	116mg	3%
Sodium	4.7mg	0%
Manganese	0.1mg	3%
Fluoride	215mcg	varies according to where the coffee originated.

Our seeds may not be a complete source for your daily vitamin needs, but it is a great way to start the day, and fuel the rest of your waking hours. We give you so much more than a caffeine jolt. And I haven't even mentioned the awesome benefits from the antioxidants and amino acids we provide. But first let's take a look at the fear mongers.

The Old Dope Peddler

There has been a curious debate for many years among some humans who are concerned about possible moral decline and health risks from drinking coffee. Some view consumption of our liquid enlightenment as a special delivery invitation from the mortician, while others link coffee with the devil. But still other voices proclaim all kinds of benefits, including 100th birthday parties and the ability to leap tall buildings at a single bound. I must say that I am shocked at some of the claims being made on both sides of the coffee cup.

While much of the negative press on coffee consumption targets caffeine, others harbor a fear of coffee that has political and sometimes religious origins dating back to some of the earliest coffee cultures, but most of these prohibitions didn't withstand the test of time and were soon abandoned. A few centuries later even the Pope, after sampling a fine Italian brew, gave it the papal stamp of approval. I think it was a cappuccino, named for the similarity in color to the garb worn by the Capuchin monks.

There have been charges that coffee consumption leads to sexual depravity in men and the moral decline of women. From my observations, this is more often the result of imbibing spiritous liquors, and the liquid remains of dead grapes.

Others argued that this same innocent and beneficial coffee diminished the flames of human passion. All I have to say on this subject is that this is certainly not the case with any coffee trees I know. In my humble opinion, coffee consumption, unlike those horrid fermented beverages, empowers the mind and the imagination. Those spiritous drinks of depravity limit a human's ability to make moral decisions. Coffee, on the other hand, enhances your decision making abilities.

Much of this scare mongering about coffee is centuries old and often based on myth and superstition rather than science and reason. This being said, there are some problems that can arise when any food or drink is consumed in excess.

Let's discuss some of these potential results of too much of a good thing. If you experience any of these discomforts when you enjoy your coffee, please check with your doctor. These can be indications of other problems, or you may simply be unfortunate enough to react negatively to coffee. It may be that you need to exercise more restraint, and indulge in a little less coffee.

Reacting with medications - This can include over the counter and prescription drugs. Before you begin taking a newly prescribed medication check with the doctor or pharmacist about possible reactions if you are a coffee drinker.

Allergies - While it is rare, there are people with mild to severe allergic reactions to coffee, caffeine, and some of the chemicals used in the production and processing of some coffees. It should also be noted that some coffee flavorings can be the source of reactions.

Insomnia - Too much caffeine can overstimulate the central nervous system. This may make it difficult to sleep. If this is the case, we advise those sensitive humans to limit their coffee intake after dinner. The good news is that it can also help keep you awake while driving, or sitting through a boring lecture or business meeting. Many humans are in tune with the Coffee-Human Connection and enjoy their coffee in the evening with no disturbance to their sleep patterns. Some claim that it even helps them to breathe more comfortably while sleeping.

Irritability - While some may claim that coffee makes them "hyper" the casual observations by this Coffee tree are that most humans become irritable WITHOUT their coffee. This is certainly the case with Hank, my research assistant who has worked with me in the creation of this informative text you currently have the pleasure of reading. I have no doubt that you are reading this with coffee, and that you are not the least bit nervous, jittery or experiencing anxiety while reading my insightful words.

Mental restlessness - Some complain that coffee makes it difficult for them to focus on one task at a time. Why one would complain about a mind able to race from one thought to another puzzles me. Being able to explore multiple concepts and possibilities simultaneous is called "multi-tasking" and isn't this a survival tactic in today's human workplace? This expectation from your job, I assure you, is not the fault of Coffee. But we do offer our beverage as a way you might be able to handle the demands of your workplace existence. An active mind is usually viewed as a good thing. If you want your senses dulled and your mind reduced to slower speeds, try chamomile tea. It is my understanding that human parents also need the multi-tasking skills that accompany several cups of coffee.

Muscle tremors - Uncontrollable shaking, often of the hands, can result from consuming too much coffee, or consuming it too fast. Slow down and enjoy the moment, and the companionship of coffee shared.

Heartburn - First let me assure that heartburn has nothing to do with your heart. It's more properly called GERD (gastro-esophageal reflux disease) and some people do experience this discomfort after drinking coffee. It's more common when the coffee is consumed black, or on an empty stomach. This is one of the reasons we helped you invent donuts. Tea can cause the same discomfort, but don't you agree that coffee and donuts is a vast improvement over tea and crumpets?

Dehydration - Because coffee is a mild diuretic, dehydration can occur, especially when the air is dry and the temperatures high. One of my Coffee friends insists that the perfect remedy is to have a glass of water with your coffee.

Rapid heartbeat - While the first cup of coffee may temporarily increase your blood pressure and your heart rate, so does running to the coffee machine for your coffee break, walking the dog when he spots a cat, or working out at the gym. Now isn't sipping your coffee while reading a good book like this, a better way to increase your heart rate than those mindless pursuits? Actually, if this does cause you discomfort, first check with your doctor. She will probably be enjoying her coffee while discussing this with you.

According to the Mayo Clinic, the problem may be Atherosclerosis. This refers to the buildup of fats and bad LDL cholesterol within and on your artery walls. This plaque can restrict blood flow. Plaque can also break loose, triggering a blood clot. Recent research suggests that coffee consumption actually helps to reduce the oxidation of bad LDL cholesterol (this is what antioxidants do) while increasing the good HDL cholesterol. If this is correct, coffee can have a positive impact on your overall heart health.

There is a certain ying and yang to the debate between the positive and negative effects drinking coffee may have on your mind and body. Research findings seem to change with the wind and often depend on who funded them and how the research was conducted. Like we teach our seedlings, "Know your limits and limitations. Smile at the rising sun and let your leaves dance in the rain. Life is meant to be a celebration."

You are a human being. You have both a right and the ability to make your own decisions. All I humbly suggest is that you make these decisions after your mind has been awakened by a little coffee, well brewed and comfortably consumed.

Coffee can be good medicine

There has been a great deal of scientific research done in the past couple decades, and sometimes the results are confusing. Some earlier sources warned about a possible connection between coffee consumption and heart disease, but recent documented research gives us some interesting results. A study tracking the health and coffee consumption of more than 400,000 older adults (human, not plant) for 13 years, and published in 2012 in the New England Journal of Medicine, found that coffee drinkers reduced their risk of dying from heart disease, lung disease, pneumonia, stroke, diabetes, infections, and even injuries and accidents.

Cardiovascular Disease - Our seeds contain antioxidant compounds. Forgive me for getting technical here, but you are a coffee drinker so I am certain you are very intelligent and can easily follow this. Antioxidants reduce the oxidation of low-density lipoprotein (LDL), the bad cholesterol. Once oxidized LDL enters the arterial wall. There it promotes atherosclerosis by causing inflammation and laying the foundation for cholesterol and other fats to build up within the artery. So, preventing this oxidation is good for you. New data suggest that an average of two cups a day helps protect you against cardiovascular disease and possible heart failure.

In a study of about 130,000 Kaiser Permanente health plan members, people who reported drinking 1-3 cups of coffee per day were 20% less likely to be hospitalized for abnormal heart rhythms (arrhythmias) than nondrinkers, regardless of other risk factors.

Scientists at Brooklyn College found that men who drank four cups of caffeinated coffee daily had a 53% lower risk of dying of heart disease than those who never took a sip. I keep telling you, I'm here to help. Now be a good boy and drink your coffee.

Stroke danger in women - I recently read an interesting article about a study involving over 80,000 nurses taking part in the long-term Nurses' Health Study. It showed that there was a 20% lower risk of a stroke in those drinking two or more cups of coffee daily, as compared to women who drank less coffee or none at all. Now be a good girl and drink your coffee.

Type 2 Diabetes - You humans seem to eat too much junk food and drink too little coffee. Numerous studies indicate that moderate consumption of coffee can be a factor in preventing or at least reducing the chances of developing Type 2 Diabetes. Unfortunately, this seems to be true only if you enjoy the coffee without the donut. Sorry.

Asthma, allergies and the common cold - These are all miserable and all too often debilitating. Coffee has been a traditional herbal medication prescribed to control the symptoms throughout recorded history and probably ever farther back in time. This isn't to say that coffee is a secret cure for the common cold, but it does give you some benefits for body, mind and spirit.

Gallstones - Fortunately plants do not fall victim to gallstones, but certainly sympathize with you humans. I have seen human friends who were in extreme discomfort when their gallstones attacked them. The good news is that a couple cups of coffee a day can reduce the risk of gallstones. In a 1999 study published in JAMA (Journal of the American Medical Association) reported that more than 46,000 men age 40 through 70 took part in the research. Men who drank a single cup of fresh, caffeinated coffee had a lower incidence of gallstones than those poor individuals who didn't drink coffee at all. I must reinforce that the benefits only applied when the coffee was caffeinated. When the participants in this study consumed another cup or two of coffee on a regular basis, the results were even better.

Parkinson's Disease - It's been known for a long time that coffee consumption decreases the risk of Parkinson's disease. But, even with the inspirations and empowerment we have provided to the scientists, you humans still have no idea why it works. Some theorize that it has to do with the caffeine, and some small studies have been conducted. The interesting results show that not only is there apparent prevention, but even some help in controlling involuntary movement and tremors with those already experiencing Parkinson's symptoms.

Alzheimer's Disease and dementia - Alzheimer's is a process in which plaque and tangles accumulate in the brain, killing nerve cells, destroying neural connections, and ultimately leading to progressive and irreversible memory loss. A fascinating study reported in the Journal of Alzheimer's Disease presented the results of research done at the University of South Florida and the University of Miami. This provides the first direct evidence that caffeine/coffee intake is associated with a reduced risk of dementia or delayed onset. The collaborative study involved 124 people, ages 65 to 88, in Tampa and Miami.

The study's lead author, Dr. Chuanhai Cao, a neuroscientist at the USF College of Pharmacy and the USF Byrd Alzheimer's Institute wrote, "These intriguing results suggest that older adults with mild memory impairment who drink moderate levels of coffee -- about three cups a day -- will not convert to Alzheimer's disease -- or at least will experience a substantial delay before converting to Alzheimer's. The results from this study, along with our earlier studies in Alzheimer's mice, are very consistent in indicating that moderate daily caffeine/coffee intake throughout adulthood should appreciably protect against Alzheimer's disease later in life."

The study shows this protection probably occurs even in older people with early signs of the disease, called mild cognitive impairment, or MCI. Patients with MCI already experience some short-term memory loss and initial Alzheimer's pathology in their brains. Each year, about 15 percent of MCI patients progress to full-blown Alzheimer's disease. The researchers focused on study participants with MCI, because many were destined to develop Alzheimer's within a few years.

"We are not saying that moderate coffee consumption will completely protect people from Alzheimer's disease," Dr. Cao cautioned. "However, we firmly believe that moderate coffee consumption can appreciably reduce your risk of Alzheimer's or delay its onset."

"Moderate daily consumption of caffeinated coffee appears to be the best dietary option for long-term protection against Alzheimer's memory loss," Dr. Arendash, a neuroscientist with the USF Alzheimer's Disease Research Center said. "Coffee is inexpensive, readily available, easily gets into the brain, and has few side-effects for most of us. Moreover, our studies show that caffeine and coffee appear to directly attack the Alzheimer's disease process."

Cancer - There is growing evidence that the antioxidants contained in freshly brewed coffee may even help prevent some forms of cancer. Please understand that preventing a disease is far better than curing one that is already ravaging your body.

I must caution you about reports from less than authoritative sources. There is a whole lot of creative misinformation out there, both in print and on line. Just because someone says something doesn't make it true or accurate. Even in the fields of scientific and medical research, new findings, often based on new techniques and research tools can provide different and more accurate results.

"Wake up and smell the coffee" is a great idea. It seems that a group of science students at the University of California with nothing better to do conducted a study on the content of the steam emanating from a fresh brewed cup of coffee, and found that it contains about the same amount of antioxidants as three oranges.

Coffee, green beans and weight control

I was reading an article about green beans for weight loss and I was frankly puzzled. Coffees have never had a weight problem and we don't eat green beans. We do enjoy having them planted around us, but that's because they have a great habit of putting nitrogen in the soil and our roots just soak it up. This makes our leaves beautiful. I asked Hank about this and he explained that what they were referring to were the raw, called green, coffee beans, not the garden variety green beans the French call haricot verts. Once I heard this, it all became clear.

Have you noticed that Juan Valdez is a pretty good looking guy for his age? We Coffees are firmly convinced that we can be a positive factor in weight control in you humans, even if you don't have a coffee plantation. I have instructed my assistant to contact Richard Simons about joining with me to do a coffee & exercise video, just Richard and me. Oh, the very thought makes my leaves tingle. So far Richard hasn't answered our email, but I understand. He is very busy. In the mean time I suggested to several of our local coffee houses that playing a caffeine enriched video of folks doing the waltz from Bach's *Coffee Cantata* would be good for business, but they have been slow to respond.

Part of the key to humans controlling their weight is exercise, and caffeine is tremendously effective in making human activity possible. It seems only natural that dancing could be a suitable exercise for you. If there was a small dance floor provided at your local coffee shop, it could provide exercise potential and be a place to find a literate and enlightened date. You must agree, the coffeehouse is a better source for romance than a smelly old bar.

There has been a lot of talk lately about the value of chlorogenic acid as a weight loss tool. This is the chemical found in green, unroasted, coffee beans. It's also found in potatoes, stone fruits like peaches and plums and even bamboo. Now you're curious, aren't you? Do pandas have a weight problem? There does seem to be some evidence that there may be a modest benefit, but you are talking about a very bitter extract that can have a laxative effect, without the intellectually empowering value of a fresh cup of aromatic coffee. I wonder if there is a similar value in the coffee leaf tea I mentioned earlier.

One of my Coffee friends suggests that a well-brewed coffee combined with the simple exercise of turning the pages in a good book, engaging in a vigorous game of chess, or walking with your new found friend can be both physically and mentally rewarding.

Your Brain on Coffee

Trust us. We have been preparing you for this day for a long time now. We have carefully nurtured your mind, your creativity, your arts, music, literature and your sense of adventure.

This is what happens to your brain on coffee. Soon after your first sip, caffeine begins to work its magic. A very special chemical, dopamine, is released by your brain and it stimulates the areas responsible for alertness, problem solving, and pleasure.

Coffee has hit the "on" switch and you are anxious to set your mind free to face the challenges and opportunities the day has to offer. Is it any wonder most homes have a coffee maker, and there's a coffeehouse on almost every corner?

A team of researchers at Glasgow University has found a link between coffee and intellect. This study seems to confirm that those humans with a passion for coffee possess above average intelligence. Our mission is to reach out to those who seem not to appreciate the delightful scents and flavors we have to offer. Around the world coffeehouses are filled with writers, artists, musicians, scientists, philosophers. But this coffee opportunity is open to everyone. Coffee drinkers aren't carded and no one needs a degree to make a pot of "start the day" coffee in your own kitchen or workplace. The coffee break is for all to relax and recharge. After the day's work, another relaxing cup of coffee is in order. It's the perfect way to celebrate the completion of another beautiful day.

You are already a part of the Coffee-Human Connection. Now, why not invite a friend to join you at the coffee party.

So you see, dear friends and gentle readers, a fresh cup of your favorite coffee isn't a bad way to start the day, or celebrate a mid-morning break, or relax after dinner, or all of the above.

Coffee is also good for the soul

Excerpted from *Tramping with a Poet in the Rockies*
by Stephen Graham, 1922.

"The lovely light of the east flooded upward and over us from Lake St. Mary, bathing our mountain-side in a peach blossom glamour; small birds winged it through the wedge of air 'twixt mountain and mountain. The creek poured more loudly into our consciousness, and the sharp points of our rocky bed jibbed upward towards our bones. Then it was morning. Then it was coffee time."

Chapter 11
A Coffee Companion on Your Windowsill

Some human experts will tell you that we Coffees are "the most intellectual members of the Plant Kingdom." We were with you on the moon. No other plant has even attempted to write a book. The truth is that we enjoy your company because you are also mentally well endowed. We have found that most of you humans seem to delight in developing a personal friendship with us. Proof that we both value this Coffee-Human Connection is right here in your hands. I wrote this book just for you, and you are reading it.

To promote understanding and communication between coffee plants and humans, I am suggesting that you try becoming a small scale cafetero (coffee grower). Raising your own coffee companion can be considered therapeutic and educational. Look at this logically, drinking coffee is considered by many to be therapeutic. So, why wouldn't living with and cultivating a seedling Coffee plant also be beneficial?

It's also good for us to have a pet human. You know, we Coffees think you're cute and cuddly, and find that most of you are capable of carrying on reasonably intelligent conversation. I have often pondered what you humans would look like if you had leaves, and I truly think you would be almost as beautiful as a coffee tree. Perhaps more important is the fact that you are dependable and remember to water us when we're thirsty.

We coffee plants are both attractive and easy to grow. In climates where frost warnings are never a part of the local weather forecast, we can be grown as a landscape plant reaching eight to fifteen feet or more in height. But for those of you who shovel snow for exercise, it's better to treat us as a magnificent house plant. It's even ok to prune us to a size that suits the space and decor. We are quite happy outdoors during warm months, but in light shade please.

There are two ways you can start a friendship with a coffee tree. Some enjoy the thrill of a sprouting seed and choose this avenue. I must caution you that our precious seeds are viable for only a short time. Make certain you plant fresh, recently harvested raw coffee beans, sometimes referred to as green beans. Please do not confuse with the legumes found in any average garden. Also note that coffee beans that have been roasted will not sprout either. The following are detailed instructions for starting coffee babies from seed.

Materials you will need to grow coffee seedling:
1. 1 coffee mug filled with freshly brewed coffee
2. 1 sandwich size plastic bag, or an empty McDonald's sundae cup.
3. Sufficient moist potting soil to fill bag or sundae cup ½ full. Don't use the cheap soil found at your friendly neighborhood bargain store. That stuff is an insult to weeds.
4. 1 part coarse sand to 3 parts good quality potting soil.
5. 1 part used coffee grounds for every 3 parts soil, brand of coffee doesn't matter
6. 3 to 5 coffee seeds (fresh green, unroasted coffee beans).
7. A deep appreciation for a fine cup of coffee, decaf or regular

Putting it all together:
1. Take a sip from your cup filled with coffee, to spark your creative genius and put you in the mood for this project.
2. Mix the sand, coffee grounds and soil thoroughly.
3. Take another sip of your coffee. You have earned it by mixing the soil.
4. Fill the sundae cup or sandwich bag half way to the top with the soil you mixed so well.
5. Now take another sip of coffee and meditate for a moment to prepare yourself mentally and emotionally for the next step.
6. Evenly space 1-3 seeds, flat side down, and press into the soil to a depth approximately twice the thickness of the seed. Cover the seeds well, wipe your hands on your shirt and have another sip of coffee to celebrate a job well done.
7. Moisten soil lightly. You don't want us to try sprouting in mud, do you? Seal the bag or put the lid on the sundae cup.

The coffee seeds may germinate in 2 to 6 weeks, but some will take as long as 4 to 6 months. The fresher the seeds, the faster they sprout. When the infant coffee plant has both the first leaves to emerge from the soil, and a second pair greeting the sun, you are ready to transplant into a 4" or 6" decorative flower pot, or a creative and uniquely yours "found container." Use the same soil mix you used for sprouting, keep the little ones watered and in a north or east facing window. We thrive anywhere you can grow an African violet.

Rescuing a growing seedling

If you purchased a poor abused and neglected little baby coffee plant at a greenhouse or on eBay, I thank you for your kindness. I, myself was a product of such an abusive infancy. It makes me shudder to think of so many poor baby coffees being produced in the botanical version of a "puppy mill." They are kept in overcrowded greenhouses. They never get to hear good music. No one reads children's stories to them. They never even get to watch Sesame Street on TV. They never hear a kind word from a compassionate human. If even thinking about such a deprived infancy disturbs you, perhaps you had better calm your nerves with another sip before starting. Good, now you seem ready to proceed.

Materials needed:
1. One large coffee mug filled with freshly brewed coffee
2. Plastic or clay pot, a creative container, or an empty coffee can with a couple holes punched in the bottom so water doesn't get trapped and drown the tender roots. Tomi and Hank first gave me a vintage blue enamelware coffee pot that was one of the props in a movie version of a Tony Hillerman novel. Perhaps this is where my dreams of starring in a movie of my own began. Now I have a rather ornate silver compote, more befitting my status as a published author.
3. Sufficient moist potting soil to fill the container. 1 part coarse sand and 1 part used coffee grounds for each 3 parts quality potting soil
4. The coffee infant you have adopted
5. A deep appreciation for a fine cup of quality coffee

Putting it all together:
1. Mix the soil, sand & coffee grounds, then pause and sip the coffee. This helps to prepare yourself mentally and emotionally for this awesome responsibility of nurturing a Coffee plant.
2. Fill your chosen container, the new home for your young coffee companion, to the brim with the soil mix.
3. Raise your right hand (can substitute the left if you insist) and hold up your thumb. Now rotate your hand so that the thumb is pointing down.
4. Then press that thumb as deeply into the soil as you can. This makes a suitable hole for your seedling to occupy.
5. Another sip of coffee is now in order.
6. If you are planting 2 or more seedlings, you can either make the hole larger and plant them all together, or you can make separate holes.
7. Place the seedlings in the hole(s) and pack the soil firmly around them.
8. Have another sip of coffee, then add water to the pot containing these cute little baby Coffee plants. The soil should be moist, not soggy.
9. You have successfully completed the first part of this project. Sit back and enjoy whatever is left of the cup of coffee that you have been sipping

throughout this process. You may need a refill. That's ok.

10. At this point, to help with the bonding process, and advance the infant's cultural identity, I suggest that you read a favorite passage or two from this book. It is a good idea to make this reading a daily ritual. This benefits both your Coffee companion and you. Remember that your young friend usually goes to sleep as soon as the sun sets for the day, so share the stories and conversation early.

Coffee notes:

As soon as possible, please give your Coffee child a name. It is important for our youngsters to feel wanted and loved, and when you are talking with them, they do appreciate being called by name. Some exceptional coffee companions will even make a creative name tag for their newly potted friend.

You can now show off your new Coffee kid to your friends, neighbors, family, even total strangers on Facebook, Twitter or your favorite social media. Place your caffeinated companion in a north or east window and keep soil moist, but not soggy. Soon you will be rewarded with more beautiful leaves.

We enjoy intellectual conversation and an occasional game of chess, but aren't very good at poker. If the TV is on, we prefer PBS. It is suggested that National Geographic and Smithsonian Magazines be kept nearby. We also enjoy reading over your shoulder, so it's best to read only the best writing. Most Coffee plants are multilingual and will respond equally well, regardless of the language you use addressing us.

Frequent feedings with your favorite organic fertilizer during the warm months will keep your young Coffee companion happy and healthy. If you aren't an organic gardener, then feel free to use your favorite balanced chemical plant food.

Don't hesitate to prune, trim and shape the coffee plant as it's growing. This makes it fuller and encourages more flowers. If you look closely at the commercials on TV, you will notice that even Juan Valdez carries a pair of pruning shears as he and Conchita roam his mountainside plantation and Parque Nacional del Café (National Coffee Park) in Columbia.

Our bright, shiny, dark green leaves make us attractive and dramatic specimens indoors or on a shaded patio. Having a coffee tree in your living room provides great opportunities for after dinner conversation, with either the human guests or the Coffee herself.

Warning! You will be asked, "Can you really grow coffee beans on that thing?"

The answer Tomi gives to this silly question is, "Of course!"

After years of care and nurturing through sickness and health; if you have led a good life and achieved harmony with the universe, you may find clusters of fragrant creamy-white flowers on your coffee companion some morning. Incidently, our delightfully fragrant flowers form all along the stems.

These flowers, if pollinated, are followed by clusters of "berries" or "cherries" that usually contain two seeds each. When ripe, these berries are red. The pulpy husk needs to be removed and the beans dried, then roasted in the oven before you can reach for the coffee maker. Sure, it's easier to purchase a delightful brew from your favorite coffeehouse, but there's a real thrill in sipping a cup of the stuff you grew in a partnership with a real live Coffee tree. Hank and Tomi estimated the cost of the cup of coffee they grew while living in Florida, to have been about $145 per pound.

I like to think that we are worth the cost and the wait.

Chapter 12

24 Uses for Second-Hand Coffee Grounds

This may sound crazy, but one of the problems we Coffees constantly face in our efforts to domesticate you humans, is the terrible waste you are all so guilty of. When we discard our old leaves or spent flowers, we place them on the ground where they will help keep the soil moist and loose as they gradually become mulch, then compost, providing food for the insects and soil organisms, then finally becoming food for the next generation of coffee leaves. It's the recycling thing, and coffee grounds deserve better than plastic bags in the landfill.

Here's a few ways coffee grounds are being recycled and reused around the world. Sit back with a fresh cup of your favorite coffee and see if you can come up with a few more uses.

1. Your hair - Coffee grounds were once commonly used to soften your hair and give it a richer color and sheen. Simply rub coffee grounds through wet hair after shampooing, and then rinse. Note: we prefer using rain water for the rinse, but some say this is just a plant thing.

2. For brown hair, coffee grounds add highlights. Men, take note. As you age and become wiser from a life long relationship with coffee, you will find that coffee grounds can darken your, shall we say, faded hair. It even works for your beard. I personally think a coffee tinted moustache is most attractive. It makes you look a little more like Juan Valdez.

3.Skin care - In some of the finest beauty spas fresh, warm coffee grounds are used as a treatment for your skin, both as a way to soften wrinkles and as cleanser. Apply gently, lightly massage over skin, rinse with warm water.

4. Coffee tan - Some suggest using coffee grounds as a way to lightly tan the body. I personally prefer the sun, but you know about plants and the sun we worship.

5. The family dog - You gave your Rex, or Fluffy, a bath and now it's time for coffee. NO, not for you, for the dog. If you gently rub coffee grounds through the canine fur coat, it will soften and add a rich shine to match the now slightly brown color. There are many who claim that these coffee grounds groomings repel fleas, mites and mosquitoes. Note though that when you do this, the canine coat will take on a darker shade, so I don't recommend this for white dogs. Nor do I even suggest that you try this with cats. Cats have no appreciation for either a bath or coffee. Important note: coffee can be toxic to both dogs and cats if consumed, so be sure to rinse the pet well.

6. In the garden - Coffee grounds are nutrient-rich, slightly acid, and make a great addition to your flower, vegetable or herb garden. Coffee grounds worked into the soil will increase the yield of carrots, parsnips and many other root crops. It is magic for tomatoes, peppers, squash and melons.

7. Composting - Adding coffee grounds to your compost bin can speed up the process and make the compost more nutritious for your plants.

8. Flowers - Colors of roses and other flowers may become more intense after you share your coffee grounds with them.

9. Indoor plants also enjoy frequent applications of coffee grounds. Tomi tells of visiting a doctor's office, and noticing the abundant growth on a plant that received limited light. When she asked the secret to this prolific growth, the office administrator attributed it to sharing her left over coffee with the plant on a daily basis. Please note, plants prefer their coffee black.

10. Soil conditioner - Coffee grounds can be added to the soil in the garden before seed planting. The grounds help to hold moisture and keep the soil loose for the sprouting seeds.

11. Grow mushrooms on old coffee grounds. The folks at Peet's coffee have been supplying coffee grounds for a line of mushroom growing kits.

12. Repel snails and slugs and some kinds of ants when you scatter them on the soil surface. When the grounds dry, it makes it difficult for them to walk across. I guess it's something like hiking the Sahara.

13. Earth worms - Coffee grounds added to the soil, or applied to the surface can increase the earthworm population. Some claim that the coffee grounds make these little critters amorous. Then they simply go about doing what earthworms are supposed to do, but now they are both more enlightened and enthusiastic. This is a benefit for the gardener and those who attempt to outsmart fish.

14. Cats, your own and those who roam the neighborhood, are sometimes tempted to use your garden as a litter box. Some cats can be persuaded not to do this if you spread coffee grounds and orange peels in your flower beds.

15. If you live where winters are cold (we Coffees choose NOT to do this) and have large quantities of dried coffee grounds available, this is a very effective way to melt snow and ice on your walks. Your lawns and landscape plants will appreciate the coffee grounds, rather than the deadly spreading of salt. Salt can seriously harm many plants and the soil dwelling organisms that make your soil healthy.

16. Air fresheners - Moist coffee grounds make a great room deodorizer when placed in a bowl, and can be even better with lemon peels or a little vanilla added. You can also control negative aromas in refrigerators and freezers with a bowl of used coffee grounds in the freezer to remove unwanted odors.

17. My very dear friend Bianca, to whom this book is dedicated, told me that you can eliminate foul odors in the household by browning some coffee grounds in a frying pan. She says this emits a most delightful aroma, much better than cooking fish, or that horrible stale tobacco smoke.

18. Onions - Sometimes human hands absorb the odors of what you are working with, like onions or garlic. If you rub coffee grounds on your hands before washing, the bad smells can easily be removed. I had Hank try this and it really does work.

19. Hand cleaner - A friend of mine who works long hours in his garden tells me that rubbing his hands with warm coffee grounds before washing them not only helps clean them, but makes the skin smoother and eases arthritis pain.

20. Pot scrubber - Yesterday's coffee grounds can be used as a mild, almost gentle cleaning compound for surfaces that won't stain. This works on pots and pans, even coffee pots.

21. Furniture scratches - If you have light scratches on wooden furniture, gently rubbing with moist coffee grounds can solve the problem.

22. We housebound coffee trees enjoy a fireplace when its cold outside, but don't like to get all the ashes on our leaves when our human servants clean. If you have a fireplace, here's another way to make good use of moist coffee grounds. Sprinkle them over the ashes before you clean the fireplace. This will help to keep the dust under control.

23. Coffee grounds can be used as a dye. If you add a small amount of hot water, they can provide a variety of shades of tan through brown for cloth, paper, even eggs. I understand that makes a background color for people who choose to do decorative painting on egg shells, and we Coffee are pleased to contribute to any such artistic endeavor.

24. Chef's surprise - Fresh used coffee grounds can also be one of your chef's secrets. It can be used as a marinade for beef, pork, chicken and turkey. Not only does the delicate and delightful flavor of coffee come through, it also serves as a meat tenderizer. One local restaurant specializes in coffee chicken and shrimp. It even makes a great seasoning for chili, gravies and sauces, homemade ice cream, cookies, cakes and a feast of other foods.

Chapter 13
Will Sing for Coffee

Throughout human history, we have tried to encourage your active involvement in music, and your use of song as a learning tool. It seems the human mind, when powered by coffee, thinks in rhyme and remembers with rhythm. For you music is a creative, sensory form of communication. And with coffee as inspiration, we have helped you humans create a lot of music. Is it any wonder that your songwriters and musicians have dedicated so many of their efforts to us?

From the previously mentioned Bach's *Coffee Cantata*, to Bob Marley's *One Cup of Coffee* and Bob Dylan's *One More Cup of Coffee*, these are only a few of the songs that celebrate the Coffee-Human Connection. These can be found on YouTube and there are hundreds more to be found in other languages and in all parts of the world. I have listed the song title, then the performer. This may not be the coffee powered genius who actually wrote the music or the lyrics. If you want to do some serious research, may I humbly suggest that you begin the quest with a cup of coffee, a curious mind and Internet access, something wisely provided at so many coffee shops.

40 Cups of Coffee, Tennessee Ernie Ford
5 Cups of Coffee, The Jayhawks
A Cup of Coffee, Johnny Cash
A Cup of Hot Coffee, The Outsiders
A Lonesome Cup of Coffee, Mel Torme
All of this and Caffeine Too!, The Vermin
Apple Pie and Coffee, Jerry Clower
Black Coffee, Sarah Vaughan
Coffee Black, John Pizzarelli
Java Jive, The Manhattan Transfer
Percolator, The Ventures
Sugar in My Coffee, Ginger Leigh
The Coffee Song, Bob Dorough
Too Much Coffee Man, Bob Dorough

Because music is one of the ways plants, animals and all humans communicate and express creative energy, we encourage the patrons of coffee houses, and those of you who simply gather with friends for a coffee party, to seize the opportunity to burst into song while enjoying your time together.

Carly Simon
Clouds in My Coffee
from Carly Simon's *You're So Vain*.

I had some dreams they were clouds in my coffee
Clouds in my coffee, and . . .

You're so vain, you probably think this song is about you
You're so vain, I'll bet you think this song is about you
Don't you? Don't You?

Carly Simon was asked by a fan, "Can you tell me what the meaning of the phrase 'clouds in my coffee' has in the context of your song *You're So Vain*? I can't quite pin down the metaphor. What are those clouds in your coffee?"

This was her response. "Clouds in my coffee are the confusing aspects of life and love. That which you can't see through, and yet seems alluring... until, like a mirage that turns into a dry patch. Perhaps there is something in the bottom of the coffee cup that you could read if you could (like tea leaves or coffee grounds)." Carly Simon 5/17/01

Clouds in My Coffee

I want to share a story about a friend of mine. It's a short story, just long enough for a cup of coffee. Zelda is old, but no one knows just how old because she tells everyone she is about to celebrate her 68th birthday. It seems that she celebrates at least a birthday a month. We all suspect this isn't quite true, because her son is 71.

Still folks will ask her to share the secret of her longevity. She smiles and replies, "I'm an addict." Then she smiles and explains that she is addicted to coffee. "Every morning begins with a cup as I spend some time in the sunroom with a good book or tending my plants." This is really where Zelda's story begins. One morning Carly Simon's "Clouds in My Coffee" was playing on the radio. She reached over to tilt her coffee cup. "I was lookin' for the clouds," she explained.

Unfortunately, some of the coffee spilled onto the white paper tablecloth. The pattern of the spill intrigued her. "Looked sorta like mountains. I took my napkin and tried to clean it up a bit. The texture of that paper napkin made coffee marks that looked to me like tree branches. Through these branches you could see the mountain range in the distance."

The next half hour was spent dipping the napkin and fingers in the now cold coffee. But, she was learning how to make different subtle shades of coffee tan and brown as she completed what she named "Coffee Mountain." This was only the beginning. In the next few weeks she tried papers of assorted colors and textures, including crushing the paper in her hands to create textures. She used coffee without cream to create dark storm clouds. Sugar sprinkled on the wet coffee gave her snow capped mountain peaks. A few finger strokes of craft glue then a teaspoon of coffee grounds became a "Road Less Traveled."

When friends visited one afternoon, they viewed a private showing of Zelda's Gallery. Soon they were also trying their hand at producing their own coffee color art. She was talked into teaching a class in her new art form at the senior center. Then one of her coffee creations won a ribbon at the county fair. This was a slightly irregular coffee cup done in coffee tones with pale coffee tan clouds floating above the rim. The article in the newspaper had the headline "No Use Crying Over Spilled Coffee." When she received the ribbon, Zelda thanked Carly Simon for the music that inspired her that first morning.

She then launched into the kind of conversation that had made her such a good teacher. She didn't talk about her new art form. She talked about Carly Simon. "She was the daughter of Richard Simon, co-founder of the big publishing house we know as Simon & Schuster. She was married to James Taylor for a few years. OH! One more thing. The name of the song wasn't Clouds in My Coffee. It was "You're So Vain."

Frank Sinatra's Coffee Song

I mentioned Frank Sinatra's *Coffee Song* earlier and feel that it is time to give you a more complete commentary on the socio-economic conditions in Brazil during those difficult years. There are numerous recordings of Frankie singing this song available, including several on YouTube. It was written by Bob Hilliard and Dick Miles. Judging from their wit and obvious knowledge of the way humans function, they must have enjoyed their coffee as much as Mr. Sinatra did.

Way down among Brazilians
Coffee beans grow by the billions
So they've got to find those extra cups to fill
They've got an awful lot of coffee in Brazil

You can't get cherry soda
'cause they've got to fill that quota
And the way things are I'll bet they never will
They've got a zillion tons of coffee in Brazil

No tea or tomato juice
You'll see no potato juice
'cause the planters down in Santos all say "No, no, no"

The politician's daughter
Was accused of drinkin' water
And was fined a great big fifty dollar bill
They've got an awful lot of coffee in Brazil

You date a girl and find out later
She smells just like a percolator
Her perfume was made right on the grill
Why, they could percolate the ocean in Brazil

And when their ham and eggs need savor
Coffee ketchup gives 'em flavor
Coffee pickles way outsell the dill
Why, they put coffee in the coffee in Brazil

No tea, no tomato juice
You'll see no potato juice
The planters down in Santos all say "No, no, no"

So you'll add to the local color
Serving coffee with a cruller
Dunkin' doesn't take a lot of skill
They've got an awful lot of coffee
An awful lot of coffee
Man, they got a gang of coffee in Brazil!

Chapter 14
Coffee Quotes

I speak for all Coffees everywhere as I share the following with you. We are, by our very nature, an inspiration to humankind, and fuel for your creativity. That you are aware of, and appreciative of this fact is evident by the honors you bestow on us in your writing, commentary and even humor. It seems that we, the Coffees of the world, are always on your mind. The following are some examples of how you view our strong, rich and flavorful partnership, the Coffee - Human Connection. And you must admit, we are in a long and serious relationship.

With your indulgence, and a cup of finely brewed coffee, I invite you to sit back and enjoy these comments by your fellow humans. This is our destiny. We inspire; you create. Together we can continue to build a better world. But, please remember, we must pause and smile along the way. Some call this pause a Coffee Break. Well named, don't you think? This is your opportunity to reflect upon and glory in your domestication. Please note that some of the following quotes do not provide the source. For a plant, I am incredibly intelligent, but there is still much I don't know. I ask your understanding on this matter and accept the fact that some things must remain a mystery, and the unknown is an adventure.

Coffee is creative energy in a cup, Lady Coffee

Historic quotes

Our efforts at domestication began long ago in the history of humanity. But since our efforts to teach you artificial memory in the form of writing were successful only a few centuries ago, we must rely on more recent moments from history to illuminate this human journey toward enlightenment.

0 Coffee! Thou dost dispel all care, thou are the object of desire to the scholar. This is the beverage of the friends of God, was inscribed in an Arabic text from the 16th century.

Pope Leo XII was petitioned to outlaw coffee, but before making an arbitrary decision, he tasted it, and found it to be a pleasant experience. *Last comes the beverage of the Orient shore, Mocha, far off, the fragrant berries bore. Taste the dark fluid with a dainty lip, Digestion waits on pleasure as you sip.*

The 16th century botanist/physician Leonhard Rauwolf encountered coffee during his travels in pursuit of knowledge. After his first sip of a strong morning brew, he wrote the following in his journal. *A very good drink they call Chaube that is almost as black as ink and very good in illness, especially of the stomach. This they drink in the morning early in the open places before everybody, without any fear or regard, out of clay or China cups, as hot as they can, sipping it a little at a time.*

We have inspired musical creativity as well as philosophy and science, from J. S. Bach's Coffee Cantata, *Ah! How sweet coffee tastes! Lovelier than a thousand kisses, sweeter far than muscatel wine!* to Carly Simon's *I had some dreams, they were clouds in my coffee.* I repeat this reference here, as it is my idea that this book be consumed in sips, with no harm in favorite flavors being tasted time and again.

Tallyrand, the French diplomat and one of the luminaries of the "Age of Enlightenment" was greatly influenced by his love of coffee. He is often quoted as saying, *Coffee. Black as the devil, hot as hell, pure as an angel, sweet as love.* This is very similar to an earlier Turkish description of good coffee, *Coffee should be black as hell, strong as death, and as sweet as love.*

Alexander Pope, poet, essayist, translator, and critic was, like his good friend Jonathan Swift, a progressive satirist and thinker far ahead of his time. Both were greatly influenced by the well-brewed British coffee of the 1700's. He expressed his appreciation of the role we played in the art of statescraft when he wrote in his epic *The Rape of the Lock*
Coffee, which makes the politicians wise,
And see through all things with his half-shut eyes.

Charles-Louis de Secondat, Baron de La Brède et de Montesquieu, commonly known simply as Montesquieu, was a profound thinker, philosopher, writer, scientist and political theorist. We used our best French roast coffee to inspire this man of profound ideas and great wit. He returned the favor by immortalizing Coffee with this comment: *The coffee is prepared in such a way that it makes those who drink it witty: at least there is not a single soul who, on quitting the house, does not believe himself four times wittier than when he entered it.*

In his work, *Treatise on Modern Stimulants,* Sheikh Abdul Kadir had this to say about coffee. *O coffee! thou dispellest the cares of the great: thou bringest back those who wander from the paths of knowledge. Coffee is the beverage of the people of God, and the cordial of his servants who thirst for wisdom . . . Every care vanishes when the cup bearer present thee the delicious chalice. It will circulate fleetly through thy veins, and will not rankle there: if thou doubtest this, contemplate the youth and beauty of those who drink it . . . Coffee is the drink of God's people, in it is health . . . Whoever has seen the blissful chalice, will scorn the wine cup. Glorious drink! Thy color is the seal of purity, and reason proclaims it genuine. Drink with confidence, and regard not the prattle of fools, who condemn without foundation.*

Napoleon Bonaparte started the day with his best friend. No, not Josephine, ME. Coffee was the true force behind this powerful mind, and ego. He once said, *Strong coffee, and plenty, awakens me. It gives me warmth, an unusual force, a pain that is not without pleasure. I would rather suffer than be senseless.*

It is caffeine alone that sets my mind in motion. It is through beans of java that thoughts acquire speed. I'm not certain who first said this, but on Facebook this same quote has most likely been attributed to Gandhi, Abe Lincoln, Albert Einstein and many other coffee inspired luminaries.

Then of course there is the famous dialogue between Nancy Astor and Sir Winston Churchill.
Nancy Astor: "If I were your wife, I would put poison in your coffee."
Sir Winston Churchill: "And if I were your husband, I would drink it."

I never drink coffee at lunch. I find it keeps me awake for the afternoon.
Ronald Reagan

Inspiration waits for you in the coffee cup

Millennia ago the wisest of my Coffee ancestors held a series of early morning discussions among themselves about the best way to bring about the ultimate blossoming of humankind. Finally, the decision was made to encourage the consumption of a drink, rather than a fruit, or bread, or a soup or even ice cream. They favored a drink in a steaming hot form so that you would be encouraged to sip slowly, pause and reflect without rushing from chore to chore. Our hope was that we could inspire you humans to achieve greatness by briefly slowing your pace and setting your minds free.

In my humble opinion, I think we have been rather successful. Don't you agree? I can't imagine any of my human fans reading this book without a cup of delightful coffee at hand. As you sip, you naturally relax and contemplate these comments. Be either inspired or amused, but please seize the opportunity to liberate your imagination. Perhaps you can create a new memorable "coffee quote."

No one can understand the truth until he drinks of coffee's frothy goodness.

Anne Morrow Lindbergh understood the value of both coffee and conversation when she said, *Good communication is just as stimulating as black coffee, and just as hard to sleep after.*

I believe humans get a lot done, not because we're smart, but because we have thumbs so we can make coffee. Flash Rosenberg

Floyd Maxwell so appreciated the power in rich, well-brewed coffee that he said, *Coffee: it's creative lighter fluid.*

The powers of a man's mind are directly proportioned to the quantity of coffee he drinks, was written by the great Scottish historian and statesman Sir James Mackintosh. He is also famous for his comment after several cups of coffee for inspiration, *It is right to be contented with what we have, never with what we are.*

Not all humans are willing, or intellectually equipped, to accept and use the power of coffee. I don't recall the author of this crude statement, but it does show how far we have to go in your enlightenment. *It's a sad tale, but true. The thrifty young student comes to campus in pursuit of knowledge, only to be led astray by casual sex, recreational drugs and the sweet aromas of the roasted coffee bean.* Quite the contrary. I think that we have saved many a scholarly youth from these depravities by our very well known role in preparation for final exams and the flow from coffee to creativity found in term papers and thesis. Think back to your college days, if that is in your personal history. Don't you agree with me?

Only one thing is certain about coffee . . . Wherever it is grown, sold, brewed, and consumed, there will be lively controversy, strong opinions, and good conversation. Mark Pendergrast, author of that delightful book *Uncommon Grounds: The History of Coffee and How It Transformed Our World.*

The discovery of coffee has enlarged the realm of illusion and given more promise to hope. Isidore Bourdon, French medical doctor, literary critic and thinker of the 18th century made this comment, that I ask you to pause and think about. I think this a most curious statement, first because it implies that you humans discovered coffee, when we both know the truth is just the opposite.

I make serious coffee. So strong it wakes up the neighbors.

A sharp perfume arose, like coffee struck by lighting. Bruce Sterling

Star Trek fans may appreciate this. *We've lost the Warp Core? So how do I power my cappuccino maker now?*

Coffee is your most popular way to start the day
Forever: Time it takes to brew the first pot of coffee in the morning

Don't drink coffee in the morning. It will keep you awake until noon.

I orchestrate my mornings to the tune of coffee. Attributed to many

The morning cup of coffee has an exhilaration about it which the cheering influence of the afternoon or evening cup of tea cannot be expected to reproduce. Oliver Wendell Holmes, Sr.

A morning without coffee is like sleep is attributed to many, but the first to say this is unknown, as is the author of *Sleep is a poor substitute for coffee.*

Mothers are those wonderful people who can get up in the morning before the smell of coffee.

Coffee is the best thing to douse the sunrise with is an opinion stated by the American quote anthologist Terri Guillemets in her Quote Garden.

And at work
As soon as you sit down to a cup of hot coffee, your boss will ask you to do something which will last until the coffee is cold. I suspect that all you humans can cite examples of this simple, but regrettable truth.

Coffee smells like freshly ground heaven. Jessi Lane Adams

Tallyrand truly enjoyed his coffee. He had this to say about his favorite beverage: *Suave molecules of Mocha stir up your blood, without causing excess heat; the organ of thought receives from it a feeling of sympathy; work becomes easier and you will sit down without distress to your principal repast which will restore your body and afford you a calm, delicious night.*

Isaac Disraeli, a writer and the only son of Benjamin Disraeli, had this to say about the coffee houses of London: *The history of coffee houses, ere the invention of clubs, was that of manners, the morals and the politics of a people.* This writer and scholar also wrote, *Fortune has rarely condescended to be the companion of genius.*

In Seattle you haven't had enough coffee until you can thread a sewing machine while it's running is the opinion of Jeff Bezos, founder of amazon.com (He was born Jeffrey Preston Jorgensen in Albuquerque, NM).

Coffee, n. break fluid, Coffee break, that is.

Jesse Tyler said, *I could smell myself awake with that coffee.*

Sir Francis Bacon was an English philosopher, statesman, scientist, jurist, all around profound thinker and author. We appreciate him, not only because he was an avid consumer of coffee, but because he respected our medicinal value. He wrote, *The drink that comforteth the brain and heart and helpeth digestion.*

Creative inspiration is found in the coffee cup

Jonathan Swift made this observation when he wrote about the travels of a gentleman named Gulliver. *Coffee makes us severe, and grave, and philosophical.* I'm not certain I agree with this. What do you think, dear and gentle reader?

Coffee is balm to the heart and spirit, Giuseppe Verdi, one of Italy's most prominent composers of opera, and avid coffee drinker.

Lord Byron, the great Victorian poet, composed this commentary on his favorite drink and how it is best consumed. *And Mocha's berry, from Arabia pure, In small fine china cups, came in at last; Gold cups of filigree, made to secure the hand from burning, underneath them placed. Cloves, cinnamon, and saffron, too, were boiled up with the coffee, which, I think, they spoiled.*

Vincent van Gogh was a Dutch post-Impressionist painter. This famous and troubled artist, was a solid patron of the café and dedicated member of café society. He commented on one reason for the existence of the coffeehouse long before Starbucks, *I have tried to show the café as a place where one can go mad.*

No coffee can be good in the mouth that does not first send a sweet offering of odor to the nostrils appears in the writing of Henry Ward Beecher, who also wrote *A library is not a luxury but one of the necessities of life.*

T.S. Eliot wrote *I have measured out my life with coffee spoons.*

Nelle Harper Lee, author of *To Kill a Mockingbird*, commented on a problem that seems common to many writers. *I do much of my creative thinking while golfing. If people know you're working at home, they think nothing of walking in for a cup of coffee, but wouldn't dream of interrupting on the golf course.*

Gertrude Stein perhaps said it best with, *Coffee is real good. When you drink it, it gives you time to think. It's a lot more than just a drink; it's something happening. Not as in hip, but like an event, a place to be, but not like a location, but like somewhere within yourself. It gives you time, but not actual hours or minutes, but a chance to be, like be yourself, and have a second cup.*

John Davis Billings writing in his popular book *Hardtack and Coffee: Soldier's Life in the Civil War* stated *The little campfires, rapidly increasing to hundreds in number, would shoot up along the hills and plains, and as if by magic, acres of territory would be illuminous with them. Soon they would be surrounded by the soldiers, who made it an inevitable rule to cook their coffee first.*

The coffee was so strong it snarled as it lurched out of the pot is a comment written by Betty MacDonald, author of *The Egg and I.*

Coffee in England always tastes like a chemistry experiment, was the opinion of Agatha Christie, one of the greatest human mystery writers of all time. She was a connoisseur of fine coffees, but, it seems, fine coffee was a rarity in her

neighborhood. She also wrote in *Peril at End House*, one of her famous mysteries, while inspired by a good coffee,
"Poirot," I said. "I have been thinking."
"An admirable exercise my friend. Continue it."

It is inhumane, in my opinion, to force people who have a genuine medical need for coffee to wait in line behind people who apparently view it as some kind of recreational activity. I bet this kind of thing does not happen to heroin addicts. I bet that when serious heroin addicts go to purchase their heroin, they do not tolerate waiting in line while some dilettante in front of them orders a hazelnut smack-a-cino with cinnamon sprinkles. ~Dave Barry

Coffee (Or At Least, The Caffeine!) Can Help You Proofread Better
The caffeine in coffee could actually help you to spot grammar errors, according to a new study in the Journal of Experimental Psychology. Researchers found that caffeine helped students to correct errors in subject-verb agreement and verb tense, However, the caffeine still didn't seem to make a difference at identifying misspelled words.

Now that I AM A WRITER, my favorite coffee comment has to be Honoré de Balzac's *As soon as coffee is in your stomach, there is a general commotion. Ideas begin to move . . . similes arise, the paper is covered. Coffee is your ally, and writing ceases to be a struggle.*

Coffee stars in the movies, and on TV
I like my coffee strong, not lethal! M*A*S*H

I've just arrived in New York City. What a place! Just smell those skyscrapers. Had breakfast at a little deli on Ninth Avenue. Cheese Danish and a cup of coffee, black as a moonless night. Hit the spot. From the television show Twin Peaks by David Lynch

We can jump to the future in Star Trek; the Voyager, Captain Janeway appears to truly appreciate our gift to humanity, past, present and future. *Coffee, the finest organic suspension ever devised.* She is also aware of the hazards in too much of a good thing when offered more. *Coffee? No thanks, one more cup & I'll jump to warp.*

Wine is for aging, not coffee was uttered by Ken Hutchinson of Starsky and Hutch.

Clark Gable observed, *I never laugh until I've had my coffee.*

Dave Letterman is reported to have said, *If it wasn't for coffee, I'd have no discernible personality at all.*

Written by Norah Ephron, for *You've Got Mail* and spoken by Tom Hanks *"The whole purpose of places like Starbucks is for people with no decision-making ability whatsoever to make six decisions just to buy one cup of coffee. Short, tall, light, dark, caf, decaf, low-fat, non-fat, etc. So people who don't know what the hell they're doing or who on earth they are can, for only $2.95, get not just a cup of coffee but an absolutely defining sense of self."*

He was my cream, and I was his coffee -And when you poured us together, it was something. One of the most famous lines of entertainer and civil rights activist Josephine Bake

Coffee drinkers have a profound sense of humor

Steven Wright pondered the question, *Do Lipton employees take coffee breaks?* and some unknown coffee comedian defined *Deja Brew* as the feeling that you've had this coffee before.

Author and TV personality Alexander King summed up the depth of the Coffee-Human Connection when he wrote, *Actually, this seems to be the basic need of the human heart in nearly every great crisis, for a good hot cup of coffee.*

We don't know who commented *Sleep is a symptom of caffeine deprivation,* but many have been given credit for uttering this truism.

Decaffeinated coffee is kind of like kissing your sister, observed Bob Irwin.

Conscience keeps more people awake than coffee.

Be a coffee-drinking individual - espresso yourself!

I bought a decaffeinated coffee table, you can't even see a difference.

Decaf? No, it's dangerous to dilute my caffeine stream.

This coffee tastes like mud! Well, it was ground this morning, is an old Vaudeville joke

I don't have a problem with caffeine. I have a problem without caffeine!

Coffee is not my cup of tea

Given enough coffee, I could rule the world.

John Van Druten, the witty British playwright who penned *I Remember Mama*, once commented, *I think if I were a woman I'd wear coffee as a perfume.* I am assuming he was unaware of the fact that gardenias are members of the coffee family, and that gardenia perfume is quite popular.

Coffee makes me invincible. But when the cup is empty, I return to mere mortal, is attributed to Terri Guillemets.

It's amazing how the world begins to change through the eyes of a cup of coffee! is one of Donna A. Favors memorable quotes.

Men are like coffee. The best ones are rich, warm and keep you up all night long.

I like my coffee like my women; hot, strong, steamy.

Coffee, chocolate and men are so much better rich.

Retirement is one great big giant coffee break.

My blood type is Folgers

All the coffee in Columbia won't make me a morning person.

Theology of Coffee

Decaffeinated coffee is the devil's blend.

Coffee in Styrofoam is against my religion. This was stated by Betsy Cañas Garmon, and I'm certain many of you agree.

Mark Helprin, speech writer and advisor to presidential candidate Bob Dole as well as a successful novelist and essayist, in *Memoir from Antproof Case*, made this profound observation on the power of coffee as a religious experience. *The voodoo priest and all his powders were as nothing compared to espresso, cappuccino, and mocha, which are stronger than all the religions of the world combined, and perhaps stronger than the human soul itself.*

Parody is often inspired by good coffee. The following is a popular example.
Caffeine is my shepherd; I shall not doze.
It maketh me to wake in green pastures:
It leadeth me beyond the sleeping masses.
It restoreth my buzz:
It leadeth me in the paths of consciousness for its name's sake.
Yea, though I walk through the valley of the shadow of addiction,
I will fear no Equal:
For thou art with me; thy cream and thy sugar they comfort me.
Thou preparest a carafe before me in the presence of The Starbucks:
Thou anointest my day with pep; my mug runneth over.
Surely richness and taste shall follow me all the days of my life:
And I will dwell in the House of Mochas forever.

A cup of coffee - real coffee - home-browned, home ground, home made, that comes to you dark as a hazel-eye, but changes to a golden bronze as you temper it with cream that never cheated, but was real cream from its birth, thick, tenderly yellow, perfectly sweet, neither lumpy nor frothing on the Java: such a cup of coffee is a match for twenty blue devils and will exorcise them all. Henry Ward Beecher

Coffee on Facebook

On the eighth day God created coffee, is often quoted in this social medium, but actually it was on the seventh day that God created coffee. We were there for what was the very first coffee break. Of course, God made it a day long event. I often contemplate, in those dark hours while awaiting the sun to power my glossy green leaves, how different the history of humanity, and Coffee would have been if only you would have listened to us instead of that silly serpent.

Coffee solves everything.

My blood type is Coffee.

Instant coffee takes too long.

Coffee is not just a beverage, it's liquid sanity.

Coffee - the most important meal of the day.

There's nothing like coffee to stimulate your brain cells.

Decaf: Used to sober up after a night on non-alcoholic beer!

We all have choices to make.
You can choose to let me drink my coffee, or,
You can suffer the consequences.

My personal favorite Facebook coffee quote is this one. *Every morning I have to hold you. I need you. I want you. I love your warmth, your smell, your taste. OHHHH Coffee, I love you.* I must confess, when I read this, I have visions of Juan Valdez, and my leaves go all a flutter.

Coffee makes the world go around.

Money doesn't grow on trees, but coffee does, and coffee is far better than musty old money.

Garfield says *Give me coffee and no one gets hurt.*

No one has done more to bring peace to humanity than Mr. Coffee.

I only need coffee on days ending in "Y."

Chapter 15
What's in the Future
for Our Relationship?

Now dear friends and gentle readers, it's time to consider an important question. Where do we go from here? Together we have come a long way in the past few thousand years. Coffee's efforts to truly enlighten and inspire humankind have progressed reasonably well, but we still have a long way to go. You have, in turn, helped to create a global presence for a modest African plant. But, in the process you have forced us to be a party to greed, slavery, environmental destruction that was sometimes inhumane, even unbotanical. You have even, on occasion, mistreated us, the tree of your enlightenment.

Still, together we survive, thrive and continue to dream. This is a great tribute to the power of cooperation, not just within, but beyond, individual species. It is when we reach out to each other, even to other phyla and kingdoms, as in our symbiotic relationship between members of both the plant and animal kingdoms, that the diversity of life celebrates its most creative expression. We are both a part of something powerful. I feel that we are at the dawning of a new age. This can be the culminating era of enlightenment, adventure, discovery and, above all a blossoming of universal peace and harmony. All because of this dynamic partnership between coffee beans and human beans. Forgive me. I couldn't resist this little pun. We Coffees do have a good sense of humor, have you noticed?

We have inspired marketing that makes coffee scented candles a part of your fragrance decor. Coffee is used to flavor ice cream, candies, cookies, cakes and I suspect the day is not far away when you will enhance a dull old salad with a line of coffee dressings. Coffee marinades, gravies and sauces are already in your recipe books. Coffee will become a popular condiment and gourmet seasoning. Tomorrow's table, to be properly set, will have salt, pepper and coffee shakers. Wouldn't coffee perfumes, colognes, aftershaves, soaps, shampoos, lotions and perhaps even deodorants be absolutely irresistible?

At this very moment in time there are coffees out there diligently inspiring creative humans to write coffee based literature. Art featuring coffee as the medium is already a part of the coffee culture. The work of master latte artists is all over the Internet.

We have seen some minor roles in the movies, stage productions and music, but tomorrow will see Coffee in starring roles. There is a rumor being passed among us coffee trees, whispered from leaf to leaf, that we are working with Sir Andrew Lloyd Weber on a profound new musical work of art titled simply *Coffee*. I have encouraged him on this effort myself.

Sometimes, when I have enjoyed an especially sunny day, I have dreams of myself as a super hero with a dark brown cape and bright, leaf green costume with coffee cherry colored letter C and a cup of coffee on my leafy chest, and the center of my cape. This is a secret, just between me and you. OK? Some less intellectual and creative plants just wouldn't understand But you humans, even as small children, frequently envision yourselves as super heroes.

Rumors abound that since we took you to the moon and powered the minds that put a go-cart on Mars, that there is a move underway to name a constellation in honor of Coffee. Personally, I think this would be nice and most definitely, well deserved.

Seriously, there is a great future in store for both of us. It will involve more specialty coffees, designed for local tastes. Single source coffees will increase in popularity as you humans continue to increase your knowledge of the beverages we provide. This is also a part of you becoming more concerned about the future of coffee, and this includes us being a sustainable crop, and you providing a fair and honorable income for those families who cultivate and care for us. It is the responsibility of every coffee plant to do our part to extend the inspiration of humankind to include a sense of responsibility for all life. This is why we are stressing Fair Trade, Organic, Single Source, and the concept of mutual sustainablity. These will be the words printed on the coffee packages on tomorrow's shelves. We hope to move from the concept of quantity to quality in the coffee preferences you desire.

For far too long you have put the burden of ruthless greed on the backs of the poor families who plant our young, tend and trim us, then harvest our cherries. The focus has been on producing as much as possible, and both the farmers and the coffee trees have been held in a state of virtual slavery even in this the 21st Century. But, this is changing as we begin to look beyond quantity in both production and consumption. We are seeking ways to help you rediscover the joy of relaxing with Coffee as a friend to embrace, not a drug to be wantonly consumed.

We, the Arabica family of coffees, by working with you humans, have put down roots around this delightfully varied planet. Each climate, soil type, botanical neighborhood, rainfall pattern, atmospheric humidity, elevation, and flow of the seasons changes the flavor of our seeds, the coffee beans you so profoundly enjoy. The ways the farmers tend to our needs, even the way they converse with us, affects the flavor. This makes possible the advent of small farmers producing specialty coffees. These can be auctioned to knowledgeable members of the industry who care more about their passion for coffee sharing, than the ruthless accumulation of wealth. We are working diligently to encourage both an awareness of the needs of the small coffee farmers of the world, and the small and independent marketers, coffeehouse proprietors, innovative concepts like the Singlebrew, Coffee leaf teas, and coffee as art. But, our greatest concern is not for us, but you, our ultimate consumer and intimate friend.

We do have some very real concerns. Global warming is putting the birthplace of coffee at risk. This can seriously impact our gene pool, and it's vital to preserve our heritage. It is important for all coffee drinkers to do your part to make the future safe for both your children and mine.

As a result of the subtle, and often not so subtle, results of global warming and climate changes, we are faced with extended seasons for insects. As we are stressed, just like it is with you humans, we are subject to diseases, infections and forms of botanical depression that, how do I say this delicately, affect our romantic life. This can limit flower and seed production, and the happiness of both coffee plants and humankind.

Mutual sustainability is the key. We have come this far by working together. The future is going to require more partnership between plant and people. This means we need to use cultivation methods that don't negatively impact the soil, water or atmosphere. We have endeavored to inspire research, and a great deal of literature is now available exploring the issues of production methods that are sustainable for us, our growers, and you the consumers. Our goal is to continue producing quality coffee for you far into the future. This is a part of our work to enlighten and inspire you.

Organic cultivation is also a concern of both us Coffees and you humans. What chemicals are introduced into our veins and leaves end up in the seeds that produce the delightful and stimulating beverage you cherish. This means that whatever is applied to the coffee trees, may well end up in your coffee mug.

We are encouraging shade growing for coffee trees. This can encourage the songbird and beneficial insect populations. This has the potential to make a positive difference all over the world. But it can also have a benefit for the growers. The overstory trees can also provide a harvest. Moringa trees could provide seeds for oil or water purification, which we strongly encourage, and leaves for food, most delightful in a salad, have you heard?

It seems that this curious tree suffers from an image problem. Moringa is, forgive me for saying this, but it's not going to win any botanical beauty contests. Coffee trees are beautiful from our deep green, glossy leaves to our seductive cherries and the allure of the fresh brewed beverage you celebrate in art, literate and song. The moringa tree proves that beauty is as beauty does, and moringa's leaves are incredibly nutritious and are saving multitudes of humans from malnutrition, hunger and starvation. But, the beauty of this tree goes beyond food to the other critical problem you are facing. Water to make coffee with, or even safe to drink, is difficult to find for many humans around the world. The seeds of the moringa can be an inexpensive, sustainable and environmentally friendly way to purify water.

I am so proud of my human staff; Tomi and Hank wrote a children's book, *Miracle of the Moringa Tree*. A woman I deeply admire, Miho Komatsu is an artist and she did the artwork for this delightful little book. I am hoping that she will someday do my portrait. This little book is about how two children save their village from starvation when they meet a talking moringa tree. This is dear to my leaves because it takes place in Kenya, and my family has roots there. My hope is that someday moringa and coffee can grow together and benefit you, me and the moringa tree.

Other trees could provide fruits and nuts for the families growing the coffee and for sale. I like the idea of diversity in the fields where coffee is grown.

As I sit here watching my words become a reality on the computer, a thought occurs to me. Coffee and people are the same color, or should I say diversity of colors. This diversity is the source of creativity and survival for both of us, and we are all in this glorious adventure together.

Fair trade for Coffee

Through our shared history, both Coffee and humans have made some mistakes. Humans have enslaved each other, shown a certain lack of compassion toward us Coffees as the source of your enlightenment. Too often we have seen careless, thoughtless abuse of the earth herself. Even today, with all the enlightenment we have provided, some humans are most inspired by greed, and this keeps many of the families growing the coffee you enjoy in a state of poverty and malnutrition. Fair Trade is a method of doing business with justice and morality. I don't like being used and abused, and I don't want to see any of you humans being mistreated either. Coffee and humans can work together to help small-scale farmers participate in the global marketplace without being exploited. This seems like a moral action on your part, but you human coffee consumers can have more and better product choices that are in line with your enlightened values. We can plant hope within the communities, families and farms where coffee is grown.

The concepts of fair trade are simple

Sit back with a cup of fresh brewed fair trade coffee, and let's take a look at what this means to us Coffees, you coffee drinkers and the families who tend the coffee trees. It even goes beyond this to include developing ways that we can work together to make coffee production both sustainable and environmentally friendly. The following has been adapted from Lutheran World Services statement on fair trade.

Fair trade is a matter of fairness. This means that together we can help level the playing field between producers from poor, remote regions of the world and big corporations from wealthy countries. This involves some things I know you care deeply about. After all, we have worked hard, for generations, to enlighten you

This includes opposing cruel working conditions, supporting women's rights and protecting children from danger and abuse. Promoting democratic principles and the empowerment of the grower families is a part of the fair trade coffee you may be sipping at this very moment. Isn't it great to be able to be a part of this effort?

There are organizations that define, promote and monitor industry participation in fair trade practices. I have listed several websites that explain these principles far better than I can. I should add that fair trade isn't only for coffee, it's also for chocolate, some teas, fruits and more. Together, you and I can make this work. Are you with me?

Fair Trade means:

Working with democratically-run organizations and cooperatives that give members a voice and the power to negotiate fair prices.

Guaranteeing farmers a fair price based on their cost of production, cost of living and the quality of what they produce.

Education is important. Every human seedling, I guess you call them children, should have access to an education. This means following labor regulations so that children are not forced to work at the expense of going to school. Human children, and their parents, should have the opportunity to learn.

Safety of the children, both human and coffee, is important and fair trade can be a part of the process of making health and safety a reality.

Fair Trade is working. It's far more than just business: it proves that compassion and integrity in world trade are possible. It highlights the need for change in the rules of conventional trade and shows how a successful business can make people, and the environment, high priorities.

Fair Trade promotes development and sustainability. This means that a portion of the proceeds are invested in the community. This can benefit both the coffees and humans who live there. This involves clean and safe water sources. I hate to say this, but it is true. You humans aren't as clean as we Coffees. You are the primary reason so much of the world's water isn't safe for you or me to drink. I know that with a a little more coffee consumption, you will be inspired to mend your ways.

Fair trade can also be instrumental in providing better education, including access to schools for girls. Health clinics, improved diets, family and community gardens and grower co-ops can all be a part of the fair trade picture. The beauty of this is that you can be a part of the effort every time you purchase fair trade coffee. This doesn't mean that you must use fair trade products exclusively, but every little bit helps and perhaps gradually, with the time we spend together, we can make this a better world. Let's give it a try.

Coffee organizations working for fair trade & sustainability

These are some valuable information sources on coffee consumption, and sustainable methods of growing and providing a decent living for the families who tend and defend our trees and children. Knowing your vast thirst for both information as well as our divine flavor, I have included this list for you to savor:

Coffee & Conservation **http://www.coffeehabitat.com/**
Coffee Kids **http://www.coffeekids.org/**
Common Code for the Coffee Community - 4C
http://www.4c-coffeeassociation.org/
Fair Trade Federation **http://www.fairtradefederation.org/**
Fair Trade Resource Network **http://www.fairtraderesource.org/**
Fairtrade International **http://www.fairtrade.net/**
How to Go Organic **http://www.howtogoorganic.com/**
Lutheran World Relief **http://lwr.org/**
Rainforest Alliance
http://www.rainforest-alliance.org/agriculture/crops/coffee
Fair Trade USA **http://www.fairtradeusa.org/**
Utz Certified - Good Inside **www.utzcertified.org**
Grounds for Change **http://www.groundsforchange.com/**

10 Coffee Books you might enjoy

One of the joys of writing a book about myself, is the opportunity to see what others have to say about such a fascinating subject. There is no way I could, in one thin volume, give you all there is to know about me, my family, our shared history and so many of the details about our yesterdays, todays and tomorrows as we continue this shared journey. I, as wise as I am, and as much as I know about the subject, even I had to consult others who have written extensively in the field. I do have to say that much of what is written could be considered more fiction than fact, but the following seem to provide reliable information. I provide these only as suggestions. There are many others out there. The simple fact is that when you sit back with a cup of good coffee and a book, you can't go wrong. Enjoy other perspectives as you expand your own horizons. These are my top 10.

All About Coffee by William H. Ukers was first published in 1922 and is available both in print and as an ebook. Though this is sometimes a boring, dated and rather academic presentation of my fascinating and exciting story, it is a great and reliable resource and I am deeply indebted to Mr. Ukers for his work on our behalf.

Uncommon Grounds: The History of Coffee and How It Transformed Our World by Mark Pendergrast tells the story of coffee from its discovery on a hill in ancient Abyssinia to the advent of Starbucks. This is a delightful, entertaining and mostly reliable guide to what the coffee-human connection is all about.

The Coffee Book: Anatomy of an Industry from Crop to the Last Drop by Nina Luttinger is jammed full of facts, figures, cartoons, and commentary covering the history of coffee from a rather biased human viewpoint. She begins late in the journey with Ethiopia in the sixth century and traces our interactions to the rise of modern day coffeehouses. Nina discusses the industry's major players, and how the lust for control and a cheap bean has impacted the lives and culture of millions of the families and small coffee farmers, with as horrendous a toll as the use of slavery centuries earlier.

Brewing Justice: Fair Trade Coffee, Sustainability, and Survival by Daniel Jaffee explores fair trade and efforts to improve the conditions of those who cultivate and tend us for your benefit. But is it working? While this book tries to make sense of a complex and ever-changing marketplace, it wisely avoids oversimplifying the environmental and social issues. Mr. Jaffee doesn't address the changes being caused by climate change and the dangers of limiting our gene pool.

Joe: The Coffee Book by Jonathan Rubinstein is just a great, readable book about the coffee culture and where it's going. Unfortunately, it addresses this from the human viewpoint and ignores our input completely.

Coffee Talk: The Stimulating Story of the World's Most Popular Brew by Morton Satin is both an interesting history of the coffee-human connection and how it continues to evolve. Morton is a foodologist rather than a scientist or businessman, and this makes it possible for him to discuss the role of coffeehouses as the place where superior human minds continue to gather to be inspired by the empowering beverage we provide.

Coffee Basics: A Quick and Easy Guide by Julie S Huffaker & Kevin Knox. They have made this little shopping guide a reference book with lots of lists. It's complete with industry gossip and a few historical facts. Unfortunately, this is again written from an exclusively human point of view, as if we have nothing to say on the subject of Coffee.

The Perfect Cup: A Coffee Lover's Guide To Buying, Brewing, And Tasting by Timothy J. Castle was written for coffee lovers everywhere. Tim is a coffee expert and he takes us on a modern historical journey through the coffee revolution in America. This is a readable account, while providing lots of details. He includes interviews with more than thirty of America's foremost coffee retailers and roasters in his comprehensive buying guide.

God in a Cup - The Obsessive Quest for the Perfect Coffee by Michaele Weissman, is a comprehensive exploration of the specialty coffee industry from farm to cup. If you want an inside look at what defines the coffee selections you humans purchase, this is your resource.

Coffee: A Guide to Buying, Brewing, and Enjoying by Kenneth Davids is a great guide to brewing, buying and enjoying coffee. Kenny writes with a sense of humor, but he knows the subject well.

About Me and My Staff

My name is Ms. Coffea Arabica (a.k.a. Coffee), known to my friends as Lady Coffee. I have been described as a beautiful, literate and profoundly philosophical plant. Still, I did not take the challenge of writing a book lightly. No Coffee tree, or any other plant I know of, has ever actually sat down and created a book before. But I felt it was time for our story, the story of the Coffee-Human-Connection to be told from Coffee's perspective. This is my first literary endeavor, but I must confess, I have already been thinking about a novel that explores the romance of coffee. As I commented at one of our editorial review sessions, "My writing is exceptional and unique. Neither this, nor any other work of fiction or non fiction I might undertake in the future can be considered your garden variety literary masterpiece."

My childhood was spent in a cramped greenhouse that was the equivalent of a puppy mill for plants. There, deprived of a suitable education for a plant so rich in tradition and global significance, I languished, dropping leaves in desperation. I was so depressed by a serious lack of sunshine, that I almost gave up. But there was a lot of fight left. One day I seized the opportunity and escaped in the shopping cart of Tomi Jill Folk, my publisher.

I have thrived in the home of Tomi and her husband, Hank Bruce. They are caring and creative book people who respect and appreciate all plants. They encouraged me to read everything I could get my leaves on, and watch PBS on the TV at every opportunity. I soon made up for lost time. I became familiar with the historical drama of Coffee's efforts and the massive global undertaking of enlightening and domesticating all humanity. I was driven to research even deeper into the history and progress of this effort. But it all celebrated the role of humankind, not the innovative and resourceful Coffees. Then it dawned on me with the first rays of a bright rising sun. All of these books were written by humans. Of course it was from their viewpoint.

Soon I became obsessed with the desire to write my own book. Tomi and Hank tried to gently dissuade me, but I was persistent. Eventually I prevailed and the result is this book. I must confess, I had trouble typing with these beautiful leaves. Finally I was able to convince Hank to take dictation and do the keyboard work for me. It has been said that I am a very demanding task mistress and I admit, I have kept Tomi up late many nights, then frequently awakened Hank at the first hint of dawn to continue my work. Being a plant means I have a deep and compulsive affection for the sun. But I have always been most generous in supplying Tomi and Hank with pots of fresh coffee during these never-ending work sessions.

I have been adamant that this be a history of the relationship between coffee and people. I also demanded that this account be written from the perspective of the Coffees of the world, rather than you humans who have been the willing subjects of our domestication efforts. I am most appreciative of the many ways Tomi and Hank have endeavored to satisfy these expectations, and I hope you have enjoyed, and been enlightened by this rather original viewpoint. Lady Coffee

Some notes on my human staff

Tomi Jill Folk is my editor. She holds a B. A.and Master of Divinity degree, and was a pastor in Minnesota and South Dakota early in her career. She is one of the founders and the president of the board of directors for Hunger Grow Away, a non-profit food security organization that promotes family vegetable gardens as a way to fight hunger, improve nutrition and control the spread of diabetes and heart disease. Hopefully I will be able to talk her into working on ways to improve conditions for some of the poor cafeteros and the struggling coffee trees in so many parts of the world. Perhaps, as I have previously suggested but do not want to have the idea overlooked, she will devise ways to grow coffee and moringa together.

She is also a photographer, poet, storyteller, speaker, writer and publisher. But, most important, she is my editor.

In 2008 Tomi & Hank were honored with a Community Service award by the Northern California Council of Activity Coordinators for their work nationally in service to senior citizens in the field of horticultural therapy.

Hank Bruce is my literary assistant. He is a horticultural therapist, hunger activist, teacher, speaker and writer. He is the former president of the Florida Chapter of the American Horticultural Therapy Association. In April 2007 he was awarded the Lifetime Achievement Award by that organization. He think this means he's old and ready to be put out to pasture. Isn't that what they do with senile old writers, he suggests? In my humble opinion, we make an excellent team and he needs to remain available for all that my future endeavors may require. He was presented with the Humanitarian of the Year Award by the American Horticultural Therapy Association in 2001, but this had nothing to do with his efforts on our behalf. Still we continue to inspire him with a pot or two of good coffee daily. He in return keeps me fed and watered and engages in invigorating conversation. I think Tomi and I will keep him around. He is a good typist; and speaks well on my behalf, plus encourages the planting of young coffee plants as intellectual companions.

Websites by Hank Bruce & Tomi Jill Folk:

Books Written by Hank Bruce
Enchanted by the Light http://amazon.com/dp/1466441747
Kindle edition http://amazon.com/dp/B00AGX6H1W

Peace Beyond All Fear, a Tribute to John Denver's Vision
"2008 New Mexico Book Award Anthology Winner"
http://amazon.com/dp/0979705738
Kindle edition http://amazon.com/dp/B009EBN5J4

Oblivion, a Novel Place to Live
http://amazon.com/dp/0979705703
Kindle edition http://amazon.com/dp/B0091HQYTE

Gardens for the Senses, Gardening as Therapy
http://amazon.com/dp/0970596251
Gardens for the Senses, Gardening as Therapy, Revised & Expanded,
Kindle edition
http://amazon.com/dp/B00ADF4AGC

Courage to Create, a workbook for writers
http://amazon.com/dp/1883114144

Books Written by Hank Bruce & Tomi Jill Folk
The Family Caregiver's Journal: A Guide to Facing the Terminal Illness of
a Loved One
"Caliente Award Winner" from Reading New Mexico.com 2009
for a "hot read that belongs in every home and library"
http://amazon.com/dp/078801434X

Global Gardening http://amazon.com/dp/0932855741

Gardening Projects for Horticultural Therapy Programs
http://amazon.com/dp/0970596227

Garden Projects for the Classroom and Special Learning Programs
http://amazon.com/dp/0970596219

Windowsill Whimsy, Gardening & Horticultural Therapy Projects for
Small Spaces
"2009 New Mexico Book Awards Winner, Gardening Book"
http://amazon.com/dp/0979705746

Along the Garden Path
"2011 New Mexico Book Awards Finalist, Gardening Book"
http://amazon.com/dp/0979705754

Seniors Illustrated, Volume 1 http://amazon.com/dp/0979705770
Seniors Illustrated, Volume 2   http://amazon.com/dp/0979705762

Miracle of the Moringa Tree, illustrated by Miho Komatsu
"2011 New Mexico Book Awards Finalist, Children's Picture
Book"http://amazon.com/dp/1460949234
The Pumpkin Parade, Kindle edition http://amazon.com/dp/B009O3DDR6

Books Written by Tomi Jill Folk
Visits with the Old Indian Storyteller
"2008 Finalist, New Mexico Book Awards New Age Book"
http://amazon.com/dp/0979705711

Stasha Dog's Secret Dream, A Hot Air Balloon Adventure
illustrated by Tomi Jill Folk and Hank Bruce
"2011 New Mexico Book Awards Children's Activity Book"
Currently available by contacting the publisher

A Love Letter

I must end this literary effort with the following. I recall reading about a French writer so inspired by his Coffee that he wrote this little love letter to her about the ways she affected him.

This, dear and gentle reader, is also how I feel about you. As you have turned the pages in this book, we have come to know each other, become friends and perhaps our relationship can be deeper than merely writer and reader.

For the Love of Coffee

It is a beverage eminently agreeable, inspiring and wholesome.
It is at once a stimulant, a cephalic [referring to the head], *a febrifuge* [used to lower a fever].
It is a digestive, and an anti-soporific [keeps one awake and alert].
It chases away sleep, which is the enemy of labor; it invokes the imagination, without which there can be no happy inspiration.
It expels the gout, that enemy of pleasure, although to pleasure gout owes its birth.
It facilitates digestion, without which there can be no true happiness.
It disposes to gaiety, without which there is neither pleasure nor enjoyment.
It gives wit to those who already have it, and it even provides wit (for some hours at least) to those who usually have it not.

Thank heaven for Coffee, for see how many blessings are concentrated in the infusion of a small berry. What other beverage in the world can compare with it?
Coffee, at once a pleasure and a medicine.
Coffee, which nourishes at the same moment the mind, body and imagination.
Hail to thee! Hail to thee!
Inspirer of men of letters, best digestive of the gourmand [one who enjoys good food]. *Coffee. Nectar of all men.*

I look forward to hearing from you, inspiring you and being inspired by you. You can find my contact information on Facebook on the Petals & Pages Press page. I hope to hear about your coffee thoughts and experiences. Perhaps we can enlighten each other.

Yours truly, Lady Coffee